*front endpapers:*
*common birch, Scots pine*

*oakwood, Dartmoor*

# TREES IN THE WILD

## AND OTHER TREES AND SHRUBS

GERALD WILKINSON

DRAKE PUBLISHERS INC.
NEW YORK · LONDON

Also by Gerald Wilkinson: *Turner's Early Sketchbook*

Line drawings by Jill Gardiner

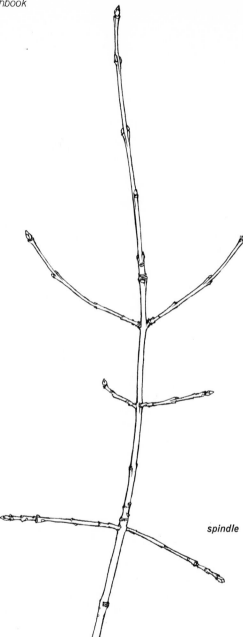

*spindle*

Published in 1975 by Drake Publishers Inc.
381 Park Avenue South, New York, N.Y. 10016
© Gerald Wilkinson All rights reserved
Library of Congress Catalog Card No. 74-22586
ISBN: 0-87749-757-5
Printed in Great Britain

# 1 – TREES IN BRITAIN

Britain and Europe are part of a forest zone stretching from the Mediterranean to the northern ice. At present ice affects no part of the land permanently, except the high alps, where glaciers still roll such as carved our mountain valleys. When the last ice receded from southern Britain, 12,000 years ago, the seas were still at a lower level than now and the British Isles formed a peninsula. The Thames was a tributary of the Rhine, or drained into the same delta system. For about 5,000 years vegetation of all kinds was able to spread overland from south to north. Its spread was much accelerated towards the end of this period when temperature and rainfall became higher than they are now. The sea level rose to sever Ireland from Wales (leaving sea ice connecting northern Ireland and Scotland) and finally separated Britain from France and the Low Countries.

By this time trees had achieved their natural dominance over other plants and covered more than seventy per cent of the land. All the plants that grew here at that time are of course regarded as native. The country was already occupied by men, as intelligent as ourselves, who lived in harmony with the animal and vegetable worlds until they began to make themselves more comfortable. The supply of caves was limited. The people made good stone tools and kept domesticated animals which must have lived mainly on the leaves of trees. The animals cropped the lower vegetation, particularly of elm and lime, which were abundant, and all shrubs and tree seedlings. Their owners lopped the trees to provide winter fodder. This, added to a cooler and gradually drier climate, was enough to reduce the numbers of some kinds of trees to a level from which they have never recovered. The 'elm decline' is a phenomenon well known to paleobotanists, and the fluctuations of hazel, suggesting repeated and increasing clearings of larger trees, are also charted through analysis of pollen preserved in centuries of peat.

**Early cultivators**

Extensive clearings were for grain crops, introduced by successive immigrations of more sophisticated peoples from the south-east. Their method was to ring-bark the trees: the following summer no leaves would appear and the rich humus between the trees could be tilled with hoes of bone or flint. It would provide cereal crops for a few years – manure, it seems, they did not understand. Then the cultivators, probably preceded by their woodmen, moved to a new piece of virgin forest. The trees would be slow to recover. Many species of plant gained a new footing. Weeds of cultivation, such as some plantains, appeared for the first time. Hazel, always present in the woods, got a great impetus from the absence of shading trees. The old clearings would attract herds of deer, or were used to graze cattle, sheep or goats. Grass would spread, tree seedlings would be eaten: and so began the clearing of Britain's native forests which continued until modern times.

The effect on the ecology of such nomadic cultivations has been underestimated in the past. It is now certain that quite small populations could make large alterations over many centuries. As people began to settle and socialise, clearings conglomerated and the earliest of them, marked perhaps by a dark yew wood or a venerable oak, became the centres for gatherings, for what commerce and rituals we can only guess. Their tree-worship survived in our May Day festivals.

Pathways on high ground (through beechwoods?) linked Yorkshire with Wiltshire and South Wales with Kent, Gloucestershire with Norfolk. Fires turned scrub into grassland. The legendary history of Ireland tells of the earliest time when there was only one treeless plain and three lakes. In other words the people who knew only three lakes, knew only one clearing. Later there were four plains and seven lakes.

**Destruction of the forest**

Since those times we have been hacking away vigorously at the undergrowth and felling trees whenever we wanted space, timber or fuel. The social history of England since the Dark Ages is intimately bound up with that of the wastes or forests, already only patchily wooded, which surrounded the settlements which became villages and parishes. The story of our trees is that of the uses which have been made of them and the repeated attempts of rulers and landowners to conserve and replace them. For on trees all depended; for half their material goods, a large part of their food supply and nearly all their fuel – turves were a second choice. The hunting of wild and semi-wild animals was a special privilege which we all know became an important sport: it is to the natural survival of the hunting instinct that we owe almost any wild land that remains, whether forest or grouse moor, bits of rough shooting, woods or warrens – or to a complex of needs which always included the chase, the hunt and the gun.

The Georgian enclosures gave us plantations and parks and, above all, hedges – a narrow nature reserve over a million miles long in a network all over the lowlands. The increase of the population over the level at which the agricultural land of the country could support it, is the history of Victorian and modern Britain, noble and ignoble. Industry and miles of housing accounted for most of the waste and woodland which formerly, of necessity, surrounded the towns. The countryside, after periods of rustic neglect, is now also 'industrialised' – or most of it – intensively farmed by increasingly mechanical and chemical means, which are as intolerant of the wild as a doctor is of tetanus. We can be proud that our small country provides nearly half our food, and still retains much of its pastoral character. Luckily for us, a lot of land is too rocky or poor for complete exploitation. Now only seven per cent, instead of 70, is woodland; but it is still a landscape with trees.

So some forest land, some woodland and scrub, some moorland, rocks and cliffs, some estuaries and beaches, remain for us to enjoy. Enjoy? This is not the place to discuss the danger of further disturbance of the ecological environment, an important element of which is the complex we call wild life. It is enough to repeat that the time has long since come when restoration, not mere conservation, is a clear necessity. Most people now work and spend their lives in an almost completely man-made world – most of us admit it is bad for us. But life is rich, we should not deny it, and there is no need for sentiment about ways of life which have passed, leaving only a charming echo of folklore, and perhaps, a feeling that something important is lost.

But how can we enjoy something we are not involved with? Not everyone has a yen for bird-watching or is keen to hike. Is the countryside just a lot of scenery, to drive through? And if not, what are we to do to restore our sense of balance? Surely, to know and understand the natural environment is the first step.

Our small country is no longer the waste land from which we grasp the necessities of life. It is like a garden – with a large plot reserved for food production, a few trees, a rockery, some open grass, some formidable sweeps of concrete, a copious rubbish tip and some odd corners where anything can happen. It is time we all treated it as carefully as most householders treat their own gardens. Obviously most of it belongs to someone else, but that is irrelevant except to determine where we walk and where we do not. Ours or 'theirs', we have a responsibility. But we have no business to interfere: not any more. The old people who used to ask permission from some obscure earth-mother before cutting down an elder tree were more sensible than most of us, whether we merely pull up a flower and leave a few beer cans, or take over acres to leave them despoiled and sterile. Plant a tree if you must, but first know the trees and how they fit into natural and man-made surroundings. Above all, leave the whole thing undisturbed, if you possibly can, to be understood and loved by our children.

**How trees grow**

All trees are just flowering plants with woody stems – elms, for instance, are related to nettles. Properly a tree has a single stem or trunk, while shrubs and bushes have several. The purpose of the trunk is to raise the leaves above other competing plants, and, unlike annual plants, trees maintain this ascendency. The tallest trees, on soils that suit them and in conditions they can tolerate, are therefore able to dominate all other vegetation, including smaller trees. They form woods.

When a tree dies, its offspring or that of its neighbours will almost certainly replace it. The 'high forest' is thus self-perpetuating. What it takes from the soil it replaces through waste materials – dead wood and leaves and the corpses of animals which live in its protection. A wood of dead trees will occur in nature only through flooding or fire or severe frost. Gales and tornadoes can bring trees down, of course.

Progressive changes of climate merely alter the composition of the forest by favouring different species – within extreme limits of heat and cold. Drying, leaching or erosion of the soil is unlikely because the trees protect the soil they grow in. A climate becoming too wet causes extreme conditions, encouraging the growth of mosses, which can build up into bog, permanently saturated and without free oxygen: trees die.

Where insects or fungi have killed whole forests in recent times, this has been invariably the result of bringing in an alien species for which there is no native resistance or predator. Very severe pollution of the air by concentrations of chemical industries can also kill woods of trees.

Trees grow, like most green plants, by using light in their leaves to

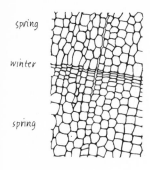

spring

winter

spring

*microscopic section of annual ring : smaller cells formed late in the season larger ones in spring*

combine carbon gas from the air with water to form carbohydrates, which they can store and circulate to areas of cell-formation. Various minerals dissolved in water from the soil are essential to the process; magnesium for instance, is necessary in the formation of chlorophyll.

Unlike herbacious plants, trees turn the sapwood of one year into the heartwood of the next, accumulating several annual rings of wood for mechanical support, and increasingly thick bark for protection, before they mature sexually and produce flowers. Pollen from the male flowers (or parts of a flower) is carried to seed vessels of female flowers (or parts), preferably on another tree to promote the genetic variability which permits adaptions to the environment.

Microscopic organisms, including moulds, viruses, bacteria and animals, live in the soil and are necessary for all growth. In the roots of trees some fungi live in biological association with the tree, providing nitrogen gas in return for their food supply. It is the stoppage of oxygen from all the soil organisms by flooding (or, as recently, by leaks in town gas supplies) which causes the sudden death of trees. Sometimes the fungi fruit above the ground as toadstools, but usually they remain unseen. Some trees in some soils manage without this fungus association, called mycorrhiza.

Other fungi are ready as soon as the tree is wounded or frost-bitten or old, to begin its destruction. Still others live on it without affecting its growth – or destroy part of it, like the fungi which can completely remove the heartwood from an old tree leaving it hollow except for the essential wall of sapwood and the bark.

Thousands of insects are concerned in the life of the tree, but so far as I know, no British tree is dependent on the work of a particular insect – as is the fig, for efficient pollination, on a particular wasp. Many insects do have particular tree-host species, and are kept in check by predators and parasites. While some trees rely on the movements of flying insects for pollination, most of our northern types are wind-pollinated; their flowering season is too early for nectar-gathering insects. Wind pollination may seem rather hit-or-miss, but remember that a tree produces a large number of flowers, not just one or two.

Mammals and birds live in the trees, some nowadays in great comfort, for their predators are extinct. No tree is entirely dependant on birds or animals to distribute its seed, but birds play an important part in long range propagation and animals which grub up nuts or eat foliage do their share in stamping seeds into the ground. Several important trees again rely on the wind.

Nearly all native British trees are broad-leaved and deciduous. Only one is a conifer with needles and cones: two others have needle-leaves but their cones are developed into berries. Three of the broad-leaved group are evergreen, as are all the conifers that we count as natives.

All our trees have two or more seed-leaves as they begin to grow and these are distinctive when visible. The earliest true leaves, which follow the seed-leaves, are usually recognisable but simpler than those of the mature tree. After the first year's growth the seedling remains as a woody stalk with buds ready to open at the proper season.

*left : beech seedling among bracken. Right : sycamore seedling with wing-shaped seed leaves and triangular first leaves*

The ability of some trees to colonise bare ground or grassland or other low vegetation earns them the title of pioneer species. Of these the birch is first. Other pioneer species are shrubs, which provide shelter for forest trees and are later shaded out or reduced in vigour. Because foresters regard shrubs as weeds they are often ignored in books about trees. But natural woodland is studied at four distinct levels : above the shrub layer is the forest canopy, below it the field layer of herbs and below that the ground or moss level. The upper layers influence the lower, some of which may be, in fact, absent. All have their typical species according to the type of soil, the altitude and climate. All have their animal inhabitants, more numerous than most people would imagine, and their parasites.

*below : rough chart based on the work of Dr H. Godwin to summarise the story of the post-glacial forest in Britain. Ten per cent of land is now urbanised ; less than this is under trees*

Each woodland pattern is a stage, sometimes the final one, in a process of natural succession – and subject, in Britain always, to a less well-documented process of human interference.

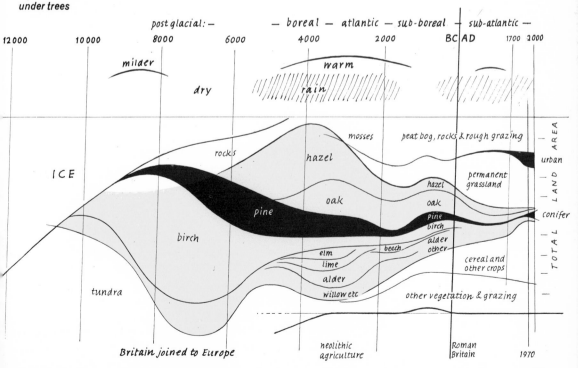

15

## Bog trees

Once, the open moors and mountainsides were woodland. These ancient forests of pine and oak were literally stifled by peat. Their stumps, and sometimes trunks, are now preserved in the thick layer of undecaying vegetable matter that lies over very large areas of Scotland and Ireland. A gradually milder, wet climate over the centuries between seven and four thousand years ago encouraged the growth of sphagnum mosses, which are the main ingredients of peat. If we had lived 3,000 years before Christ instead of 2,000 years after, we should not have known open moors and bare mountainsides, but picturesque, dying woods of oak and pine, interspersed with mires and covering half of Britain, including most of Ireland.

*above : bleached remains of pine trees (and white stones) revealed by turf-cutting in Connemara*

Early upland settlers also cleared the trees, and the soil not affected by moss gradually became more acid as the minerals accumulated during glaciation were leached out by the rain. The climate cooled; and the trees were gone for good from the high land.

*right : bog trees cut from the peat by the work of a mountain river in Wester Ross*

16

## Ancient forests

*above : an island formed in the same river in Wester Ross, crowded with pines, heather and ferns. For miles around there are no trees. The banks of the stream provide drainage and keep away grazing animals*

In historic times patches of woodland crept back as the land dried out in a more moderate climate. The pines at Ben Eighe, the large Rothiemurchus forest of pine, birch and juniper under the Cairngorm, the pinewoods near Loch Rannoch, and other fragments, give some idea of what the northern countryside must have been like. Most of the surviving trees were cut down: for fuel, to clear the land for sheep, and for charcoal used in early iron works. A more romantic reason sometimes given is that the woods were removed to clear the land of robbers and highwaymen – an early form of defoliation.

The woodlands will not return while the moors and mountains support their maximum of sheep and deer. These animals simply eat the seedlings. Burning of grass, bracken, heather and gorse also discourage regrowth. Scots pine, the native tree, is said not to grow in peat. The foresters plant spruce, which *will* take, first scraping the turf into deep fissures.

In western Scotland, and just off the moors everywhere, the vigorous growth of mature trees is very striking in well-drained places protected from grazing animals. Some changes might be possible to the sour and barren moors. Of course, we love the windy open spaces : but perhaps we could do with a bit less ?

*above : on the north-east shore of Loch Lomond alders are well established in spite of being in the water when the lake is full. Other trees cannot grow in such conditions*

*coppiced alder wood on marshy land. Poles are cut to ground level every few years*

# 2 – TREES FORMING WOODS IN BRITAIN

*male catkins of alder in March, over a foaming Welsh river*

## ALDER

The alder is adapted to growing half in water and half out. It has two distinct watery habitats. The first is in marshes, which it can eventually take over, forming, with rushes, reeds and sedges a type of wet woodland called alder carr. This type of country was once very extensive in south-eastern England and in the wide valleys of many rivers which are now controlled or reduced, or both.

Alder carr with its thick undergrowth soon raises the land above water level. The result is that flood water has to go somewhere else. So once drainage of large areas of flat country was under way the trees had to be removed. Small woods of alder in the Fens, with willows, birch and alder buckthorn, are still called carrs.

The second natural habitat, most familiar in the north and west, is along the middle reaches of rivers – perhaps sometimes as the remains of swampy carr now turned into rich meadows. In mountain river valleys too, alders will be found rooted amongst the stones, and sometimes alder woods climb the valley sides. But they are never far from water.

The timber of alder is very resistant to moisture and it does not split easily: this is true of oak and elm, but while they are heavy alder is reasonably light. It is used for broom heads and other turnery and it was the best wood for

*leaves and spent seed
'cones', which remain
on the twig*

*a Scottish alder trunk
shows the clear dark grey
in un-polluted air. The
white flecks are lichen.
Right : leaves and fruits
in an early autumn gale,
Berkshire, Thames-side*

clogs which not long ago were worn by millworkers, farmworkers and miners in Lancashire. The clogs had black leather uppers nailed to the soles, which were protected underneath by bent iron strips. Most of the wood came from Wales where the trees were bought, felled, logged and cleft and shaped into rough blanks, by itinerant cloggers.

Poles of alder, being water resistant, are used to strengthen the banks of rivers, and this in fact is what the alder tree does, less tidily. Because water cuts off the supply of free nitrogen essential to plants, alder roots adopt a particular bacterium which supplies the nitrogen as part of its life process. Nodules on the roots contain the bacterium, as in leguminous plants. Most other trees are dependent on bacteria in the soil, and will die if the land is flooded, and thus deprived of oxygen.

Charcoal from alder wood was used in making black gunpowder. The bark was used for tanning. The wood when stripped or cut is bright orange and was the source of dyes – and of a powerful emetic. Says a herbalist of 1800: 'the middle bark, particularly the root, is vomative when it is fresh; when it is dry it is purgative; the bark is separated in the Spring time, and dried in the shade; 1 drachm in powder is a dose . . . the country people use it in intermittent fevers with success, because this remedy purges and vomits them vigorously, and carries off the disease'.

Woods of alder were grown as coppice. Most of the alder trees we see have been coppiced at some time and have therefore several stems – but I think the natural tendency of the tree is to spread over the water by means of low branching stems, even though its shape in ideal conditions is tall.

*an alder in winter,
Bedfordshire*

As firewood alder is poor: but it was used. If you have a log fire, a slow log can be useful to keep it in during the day. And some could afford no better.

The old English name of alder was alor, later aller and even owler. In this form, without the 'd', it became part of many place-names in England of which my favourite is Alrewas (alder-wash) near Burton-on-Trent. Gerard, the compiler of the *Great Herbal* in the sixteenth century, called it the Black Aller. Often it does look black, with its dark leaves and black empty seed 'cones' against the bright water.

*the bright colour of an alder recently cut down in an Irish conifer plantation. Shoots will grow from the stump*

At one time, in Ireland, no one was allowed to cut down an alder because of superstition about its 'bleeding' – and perhaps because it had a special place in half-forgotten legends. In another mythology, the Norse, the first man and woman were supposed to have been made out of an ash tree and an alder respectively.

The seeds, or nuts, will float, as one might expect, and are often carried down river – though this doesn't explain how the alders are able to spread upstream. The very beautiful male catkins come out in March, before the leaves. The female catkins are at first hard and green. As they ripen they become brown and scaly with the ripening fruits. They become woody: in autumn the little nuts fall, leaving the empty cones to blacken on the tree.

The seed-leaves are lobed. The seedlings do not grow in dry soil or shade. Another species, the Italian alder, with pointed leaves, will grow in these conditions and is planted in parks. There are hybrids with this and with the grey alder, another European species. Varieties with deeply cut leaves can be seen by the lakes of grand houses.

The scientific name of alder is *Alnus* and the specific *glutinosa* refers to the leaves which are slightly sticky. It is of the same family as the birch.

Alder flies, whose nymphs are well known to fishermen, are not dependant only on the alder though they often lay their crowded upright eggs on the leaves. These and other insects which drop from the tree are a major part of the diet of such fish as trout.

*dark buds contrasted with the sturdy light grey twigs are the certain recognition feature of the ash. The forking twig results from damage to the central bud*

# ASH

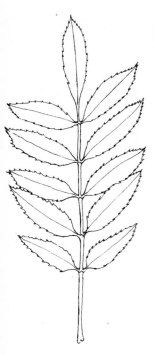

Ash wood is very strong, and ash trees until quite recent times had magic properties. For these reasons the tree has often been allowed to grow up from the hedge even though it is very demanding of the soil. The ash is most familiar in the shape of these isolated trees along the roads of most country areas. But there are many pure ashwoods, unique to Britain, on outcrops of mountain limestone, particularly in Derbyshire and North Yorkshire, and here and there in Scotland. In addition ash trees are found amongst other pioneer species as part of the process by which woodland takes over scrubland, described on page 28. The ash as hardwood is third in economic importance, after oak and beech, so we may also expect to find cultivated woods. Often these are coppiced, for poles of ash are most useful for a variety of purposes. So in all there are four distinct habitats, two controlled by man and two more or less natural.

In early summer ash trees are noticeable because they are the last to come into leaf. *Ash before the oak and we shall have a soak,* says the well-known rhyme. But even in quite wet summers I have not noticed ash trees in leaf before oaks.

The purple flower clusters, often richly covering the whole tree, appear in early May, before the leaves. The flowers on one tree can be of either sex or hermaphrodite, or all three. The twigs are thick, flattened at the leaf joints, where the black buds are set opposite and at right angles to the next pair. This rugged construction characterises the whole tree, while the foliage it carries is light and open, not resisting the wind from any direction. A tendency to fork symmetrically is due to damage to the terminal bud, by caterpillars or late frost on the opening leaves.

The leaves, of usually eleven leaflets, are often up to a foot long. Bunches of winged seeds, called keys, remain on the branches after the leaves, until distributed in winter gales. Most of the seedlings are eaten by rabbits.

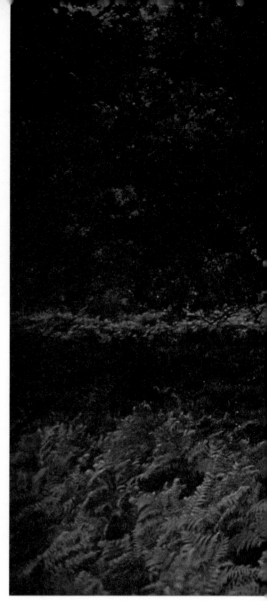

*a northern ash wood*

*left : the limestone boulders in which the wood is growing. Below this : a wild strawberry under the trees. Right : old trees and bracken*

Ash trees multiply in the rich soil which accumulates in the cracks of mountain limestone, forming pure ashwoods. The only other trees will usually be hawthorn and hazel. In the limestone country round Dovedale – the area known as the White Peak – the number of small woods remaining in this beautiful countryside of white walled, undulating fields suggests that it may once have been entirely covered with ashwoods, as is the steep valley of the Dove itself. The famous limestone rocks near Ingleton, Yorkshire, are much less wooded, but we do not know how much was felled for fuel – nor how many trees suffered by having their leaves stripped to feed cattle through the winter. Some limestone pavement on the Kent estuary provides the classic ashwood habitat, while southern examples can be found in the Mendip Hills of Somerset.

The photographs above were taken in Rassal ashwood in W.Ross – said to

be the most northerly ashwood in Britain. Within the wood a small area is enclosed in rabbit fences and shows an astonishing transformation of the bleak mountainside. Long grass and flowers form a sort of jungle between the gnarled and lichened trees, which cast little shade. The wind is cut off and the atmosphere is warm and scented with meadowsweet – at least, it is in summer. Outside the fence the floor of the wood is mostly of picturesque boulders completely green with moss, but there are patches of level soil where very green grass, close cropped by the sheep, stretches like a garden lawn between clumps of bracken. It is clear that the wood owes its survival to the heaps of boulders and ankle-twisting 'grykes' in the rock, where seedling trees can grow unmolested. The twisted shapes of the older trees may be partly due to casual lopping. The wood is now a National Nature Reserve.

*ash in flower, and
right, ash keys*

In the moister climate of ancient Britain ashes were common, and, it is thought, much larger than is usual today. The Norse 'tree of life' was an ash, its crown in heaven and its roots in hell. Later Scandinavian invaders of Britain believed that the first man had sprung from an ash.

Classical herbalists recommended the juices of the bark as an antidote to snakebite. Such myths, and an awareness of the natural strength and usefulness of the tree, are mingled in English folklore, giving the ash magical powers of healing and protection. Its sturdy growth could be transferred to a child whose limbs were not strong, by a rite which is described by several authors. A young ash tree was cleft down the trunk and the two parts held back by strong men. In the dark before dawn, the poor child, naked, was passed three times through the cleft. This had to be repeated for three mornings. The tree was then carefully bound up and sealed with mud. If it grew soundly, so would the child. The magic usually seems to have worked, for Gilbert White, writing in the late eighteenth century, tells of a whole row of trees so split and bound, and they had been used more than once.

**Shrew ash**

Ash twigs, laid in a circle round you as you slept, would be impassable to adders: a twig bound to your body protected you from the deadly bite of this once common snake. If cattle went lame this was thought to be caused by the bite of a shrew. An (innocent) shrew was therefore imprisoned in a hole bored into an ash tree, and sticks from the 'shrew-ash' were used to drive the cattle – tapping their legs would keep the lameness away.

The juice from an ash branch was given to new-born babies in Scotland. The juice, and a brew from the bark, were generally prescribed for everything from plagues to sore throats – but this was not all magic, for modern herbalists say that the bark contains the effective element of quinine.

Culpeper recommends the lye of the ash for bathing your head, if scabby or scaly. Water distilled from the leaves was a 'singular medicine for those

*hedgerow ash tree in early leaf, Buckinghamshire, end of May*

that are too gross or fat' – and you could eat 'the kernels within the husks commonly called ashen keys . . . they prevaileth against stitches and pains in the side proceeding of wind.'

*Ashen tree, ashen tree, Pray buy these warts of me,* was a rhyme you had to sing while sticking a pin, first into your warts and then into the tree. It is probably as good a way of removing warts as any.

The strangest survival of the belief in the ash as a masculine symbol, was a game played by girls. A bundle of twigs was bound with thongs of green ash; one thong for each girl was given the name of her boy. The bundle was put in the fire. According to the order in which the bonds gave way, the girls would know when they would be married.

Ash keys can be pickled. John Evelyn's recipe is short: 'pickled tender', he says 'they afford a delicate salading.'

**Pioneer trees**

Scrub – really the same word as shrub, but slightly derogatory – is the name given to a type of countryside somewhere between grassland and woodland. The tendency is for one shrub to dominate. Oak can form scrub in situations where its growth is limited by winds or low temperatures. The most common shrub is hawthorn, nearly always present in hedges, which are a sort of scrub in themselves. On some sandy or heathy ground a scrub of gorse is well-known. It is sometimes invaded by birch as the first step in the slow change to woodland. Usually hawthorn and gorse scrub are subject to continuous grazing and change is unlikely. Blackthorn, another armoured shrub, can also hold its position on cropped grassland.

On the chalk hills of southern England patches of scrub are familiar. They may be locally hawthorn, juniper, dogwood, elder and even box. Scattered shrubs will include spindle, privet, buckthorn, maple, whitebeam and the wayfaring tree. Traveller's joy grows over everything. Amongst the small trees ashes are common and it is the ash which grows above the scrub and begins the natural conversion to woodland and eventually beechwood.

The picture above shows ash trees which have been allowed to grow over old coppiced hazel. The ground is chalky and at the edges of the wood are calcicolous trees like the wayfaring tree and maple. The ground under the hazels is thickly covered with dog's mercury, which gives way to bracken in a cleared area. There are small oak trees and a good deal of elder. The presence at the edge of the wood of two enormous beech trees suggests that the whole wood may once have been beech, cleared and planted with the classic combination of oak and hazel. Most of the oak is gone, but the ashes are vigorous. According to the 'laws' of natural succession they should eventually subdue the hazel and prepare the way for the return of the beeches.

*above : ash trees in scrub, January*

**Ash timber**

The great practical virtues of ash wood are strength and resilience. As Evelyn wrote in 1662; 'the farmer cannot be without ash for his carts, ladders and other tackling, from the pike, spear and bow, to the plough'. Even in these days of steel and aluminium there are many implements that cannot be well made without ash for handles. Heavy hammers and hand axes need ash handles. Felling axes are now usually in the American pattern which originally had handles of 'dog-leg' hickory. Billiard cues should be ash, so should oars. The handles of most garden tools are best made of ash – some rakes are still made entirely of the wood, the handle split and bent and even the teeth produced by forcing small wood through round holes in a piece of iron. The great cogwheels of windmills were often of ash. Coachbuilders needed ash wood, not only for its strength in small sections but for its capacity for bending, when steamed, into complex curves. The coach builders' craft was applied to cars – up to the end of the vintage era (1932) even cheap cars had ashwood frames.

Great ash trees are recorded. One at Dumbarton is described by the Rev. Jones, writing in 1840: 'four feet from the ground it measured 34 feet in circumfrence. It was hollow and inside a room had been made, big enough to seat eighteen people round a table. There was a door with a window over it'. I wonder what would be the rateable value of a large ash ? Weeping ashes were popular and can be seen in many ornamental parks. The parent of all the weeping ashes was said to have been found in a field belonging to the Vicar of Gamlingay, Cambridgeshire, who exported grafts to Europe and America. Jones tells of a pub in 'New Road, London' – there are several such roads – which had, in the garden, a large weeping ash trained over trellis work, covering fourteen tables and benches. I am sure I have seen this tree just as he describes and over 100 years later. If there is one thing, apart from their size, that sets trees above other plants, it is their longevity, reaching over so many generations of man.

The generic name of the ash is *Fraxinus* and the specific name of the common ash is *excelsior*. The family includes the olive and privet.

*unusual fasciated twigs of an ash near the west coast of Ireland – cause unknown*

smooth light grey bark is
characteristic of the beech

# BEECHWOODS

male flower consists of
from eight to sixteen
stamens

Queen Victoria is supposed to have insisted that 'coals' for the palace fires
were made from trees at Burnham Beeches, near Slough. These trees,
distorted by centuries of lopping and regrowth are typical of many old woods
near London. Dozens more must have been uprooted and built over. In
addition there are about 25,000 acres of beech – tall forest, not ruined
coppices – within an hour's drive from London. Their presence is mainly due
to the furniture industry. The work of the chair makers was done half in the
woods, the 'sticks' being turned on open-air treadle lathes. These men and
their masters were careful not to use up the wood faster than it grew.

Now their trees are tall – the last chair bodger retired a few years ago. The
National Trust protects some of the woods, others are still managed for
timber. Beech is next to oak in value and, sawn instead of split and turned, is
still a basic material of furniture – not always visibly. Much of the wood is
imported. The greatest concentration of beechwoods is on the Chiltern Hills.
The trees thrive as no other on the steep escarpment of the chalk, their long
roots exposed on the shallow soil. But they reach their most majestic heights
on the plateaux above, where the chalk is overlaid with deeper soil. Beech is
not exclusively a calcicole: it will grow on many well-drained soils. In the
northern part of Epping Forest it shares the gravelly ground with hornbeam;
at Burnham Beeches there is gravel, little chalk. There are many beech
plantations all over Britain, often far from chalk or limestone. Ancient
pollard trees are a feature of old common land in the south-east, often at
lane sides where people had the right to 'fair loppings'. There are old pollard
beeches in the New Forest, on common land.

Beechwoods remain on all the downs and in the Cotswolds often as
preserved 'hangers', surrounded by sheep pasture or, more frequently now,
by smooth arable fields. There are impressive beech hedges in north

opposite : a giant beech,
survivor of an old forest
near London

*unfolding leaves in May.
The leaves later lose their
pale colour and downy
edges*

*the husk of the fruit
reflects the shape of the
female flower*

**Forest climax**

Somerset and high beechwoods near Buxton at over 1,000 feet. Lines of
beeches as shelterbelts have been planted in northern England and
Scotland: the tall trees not their usual grey, but green with algae or white
with lichens. Beeches in large plantations in the lowlands of Scotland as far
north as Aberdeen are a surprise to the Southerner.

A plantation usually has trees of noticeably similar ages, while a natural
beechwood – or any other wood – is marked by the dissimilar ages, shown by
thickness of trunk. A wood which has been left alone will also have its share
of dead trees. The high beechwoods, though they have an immemorial look
about them, have usually grown up from trees which were once regularly
cropped at an age convenient for making logs which could be cleft and
shaped for the turners. Trees of more than 200 years are said to be unusual.
Some giants were, no doubt, left as parent trees. There is no reason to
suppose that many present-day beechwoods are not on their original native
sites.

Ecologically the beech, as our tallest forest tree, forms the climax of a ,
natural succession described by Tansley: 'from grassland through scrub
sometimes with ash; then oak, the native tree of widest distribution and
most adaptable habit.' Beeches will grow in the shade of oaks when the soil
suits them, and there is nothing to stop the eventual formation of a pure, tall
beech forest which is self-perpetuating. The shade is too deep for other
trees to regain dominance. Certain types of scrub – box and juniper – are
directly colonised by beeches.

Natural clearings, caused by dead trees, are quickly filled by wind-seeded
annual herbs or by brambles, usually present in creeping, flowerless, form
on the beechwood floor. Seedling beeches, which start everywhere in the

*beechwood on a Chiltern outlier—edged with scrub-ash and whitebeam. Some scrub has been cleared. Saplings of beech are already growing up amongst the ash*

dark woods but normally end as crackling twigs, here get their chance to grow up through the plants which filled the gap; sometimes they are accompanied by the odd yew, holly, or cherry, seeded by the birds. The evergreens can grow easily in the surrounding shade; the cherry can overtake the sapling beeches and reach the hundred-foot-high canopy to take its share of the sunlight.

At its edge, the beechwood expands over the scrub with the help of jays, pheasants, mice, and squirrels, until it reaches soil too heavy (or more usually, farmland). It will gradually advance through adjacent mixed woodland until, on less favourable soil, it fails to compete. This is the textbook situation and you may test it in action anywhere along the Chilterns, where a great variety of scrub (identified elsewhere in this book) occupies the more exposed escarpments – and woodland of various types besides beech can be found on the plateaux and the dip slopes.

**Neolithic mystery**

The early history of the beechwoods is confused and open to conjecture: their distribution, at least in England, in the period immediately before the Roman occupation, is almost as wide as the present planted distribution. The massive pollen deposits of other common trees, which are preserved in peat, are, in the case of the beech, absent, for its most favoured habitat is the chalk. Pollen is, in any case, not over-abundant and is likely to remain within the confines of the beechwood where gales are subdued. There are widely scattered macroscopic remains.

Our present intergalacial period was well advanced, by six or eight thousand years, before the beech became established in Britain. By this time the country had been invaded by farming peoples, and no one really knows whether the beechwoods or the farmers came first. The largest

*a naturally regenerating
beechwood from which the
older trees have been
removed—showing the
light but pervasive shrub
layer*

pollen deposits, up to ten per cent of all trees, are at the extremes of the
southern chalk and limestone, where low (peat forming) country is adjacent
to the hills: to the N.E., near Thetford: to the S.E., near Bognor; to the west, in
the Somerset Levels. In the last area the pollen records are substantiated by
Bronze Age trackways containing beech poles. Earlier pollen deposits have
been identified in the Hampshire basin, dating from the dry Boreal period
when the Channel was still narrow at this point.

Small, but quite significant, pollen and macroscopic remains of the
Bronze and Iron Ages are located at short distances from river mouths: near
Middlesborough, near Goole on the Humber, in Chat Moss not far from the
Mersey, on the Cam, and near the Severn estuary, near Swansea. There are
other small finds in S.Wales, in Derbyshire and Yorkshire and in East Anglia.

These are not areas usually considered natural to beeches: how closely
they are connected with archeological research I do not know: did the
people who settled inland from the river mouths and who certainly brought
cereal crops, also plant beech trees? Some present day beechwoods in
northern France in the Pays de Bray, are not far from the mouth of the Seine.

Pollen remains are absent from the Chilterns and the North Downs, as I
have said. The Thames basin and the Medway were just as popular as
settlement areas as other ports of entry and if the hills were at least as rich
in beechwoods as they are now it is surprising that no remains are
discovered. But the downs cannot have been entirely bare and climatic
conditions were not so different from ours. It is the nature of beech to

in an old beechwood the floor is covered only with dead leaves. The soil is shallow in this escarpment wood and the roots of the large tree are partly above the ground. Only fungi, which grow without chlorophyl, and other saprophytes, such as some orchids, can survive in the deepest shade. Bramble is always present where the light increases

leaves of a young beech are spread widely to catch all the light that is available

dominate and of beechwoods to persist, even if temporarily cleared. With beeches at more than ten per cent of all trees in the low chalk hills of East Anglia, would they not be thicker still on the rest of the chalk? But there is no proof. Many ancient burial sites on the chalk hills are undisturbed by the roots of trees.

We do not know whether to imagine the busiest highways of early Britain as a series of clearings and pathways through tall, dark beech forest, or as bare grazed downs with patches of scrub and isolated woods of beech or yew. All that is certain is that the lowlands were thickly covered with mixed woodland, of which the dominant tree was usually oak but frequently alder in large areas of swampy ground. The fauna included dangerous animals, and the general effect must have been of jungle. Beechwoods, with their typically uncluttered floor of dry leaves, would be attractive to the traveller. The ancient routes on the downs are usually on the hilltops. Along the Chilterns the Icknield Way follows the escarpment – below the present woods and above the plain.

Place names including the Old English *bece* or *boc* are difficult: the many Bucklands apparently refer to charters, other 'Bucks' to persons named Bocca or to deer or even box trees, never apparently to beeches, even in that stronghold of beeches, Buckinghamshire. The German *Buche* for beech is supposed to have given its name to books because beech boards were used for bindings: as we say 'hard-back' perhaps?

From bookbindings to mangle-rollers, beech timber has always been very

yew tree in a beechwood. The yew flowers and puts out new shoots before the beeches are in leaf

below : a spider hangs in the permanent shade

below : the distinctive colour and sheen of the bark of a wild cherry, one of the very few tall trees that can invade the beech-wood

below : Lycoperdon pyriforme *fungus on a rotting branch in an old clearing. Leaves of woodruff*

*leaves of a beech hedge stay red on the twig through the winter*

useful. It is light and pleasant in texture, flecked with warm brown and always recognisable even though it is often stained to resemble other woods. It is moderately hard, even-grained and lends itself to carving and to bentwood furniture. Toys and musical instruments use beech and a large range of bowls and platters ('treen') was made from it before the day of mass-produced china. Wooden spoons today often show its grain. A lot of wood, too, went down the Thames for London's fuel, no doubt as a by-product of the chair-making industry.

The triangular nuts of the beech shared the name 'mast' with acorns and were valued as food for fattening swine. The leaves were once used for bedding – they would last several years in the mattress and being slightly toxic, discouraged pests.

*darkest of the 'copper' beeches is this variety,* purpurea, *here seen over the soft colours of meadow grass at Kenwood in N.W. London*

*a group of old pollard
beeches near Epping, Essex*
The beech is *Fagus sylvatica*, closely related to the oaks and chestnuts. It grows all over Europe and Asia Minor. An American species *F. grandifolia*, seems, from photographs, to be even more impressive than the European beech. New Zealand and South America have several species of *Nothofagus*, the southern beech: some have leaves resembling oak.

Fern-leaved beeches are grown in parks and arboreta, and copper beeches are frequent in town parks, pigmented in various degrees from red to purple. This is a natural sport, selectively cultivated.

Ordinary beech trees growing in the open begin to branch fairly low on the trunk and form a great rounded crown composed of horizontal layers of foliage. In proportion the tree is at least as wide as it is high. Grown as a hedge, the form becomes intricate, full of sculptured elbows and small twigs. The leaves do not fall from hedge trees or juvenile trees in autumn, but remain red until the following spring – some older trees keep the habit.

*fern-leaved beech*

*apparently tender and
often drooping, the twigs
of the birch are in fact
as tough as wire*

# BIRCH

Everyone recognises the birch, which grows all over Britain as well as the rest of Europe and the Northern Hemisphere. It is not merely native to Britain: it was the first tree to follow the melting ice, as has been proved by samples of fossil pollen from many different localities. It will grow on almost any soil, but is less common on the midland clays than elsewhere and even rare on the lowlands round the Wash. Birches are not much planted in Britain except for ornament. There is enough natural growth of the tree for the use that is made of it, and in Britain it seemingly cannot produce the straight, well rounded trunks that in Scandinavia and Finland are so valuable for plywood.

Thickets of birch will appear on any vacant soil where there is good light, (and no cattle, sheep, pigs, goats or ponies). As they grow the healthier saplings shade out the weaker and soon the delicate pattern of birchwood appears, with its typical floor of bracken or grass. Other vegetation is kept low by the wiry twigs whipping in the wind. But birches do not live long, usually less than a century. Quite young trees can be attacked by the special heart rot fungus of the birch, especially if they are damaged. Where they grow on watery land, the roots can be attacked by the killing honey fungus.

*birches on the banks of
Loch Maree, W. Ross, in
late summer*

The shade of the birchwoods is not deep, but it is enough to discourage regeneration. Oaks, and, in the mountains, pines, are likely to take over. So the birches are constantly – but vigorously – shifting their ground. Some birchwoods seem to be more or less permanent; in the S.E.Highlands, and, in more open, scattered form, on the few heaths and sandy commons that remain in England, notably in Sussex.

Botanists recognise two main species of birch in Britain, but these shared the same name in Linnaeus: *Betula alba*, the white birch. The two are so similar that only close examination of the twig will tell them apart (and even then you may find you have the hybrid). They are, *B. verrucosa* (warty) or *pendula,* the silver birch; and *B. pubescens*, the hairy or common birch. A third species is *Betula nana*, the dwarf, a low shrub, the only native tree in Greenland, and confined in Britain to the mountains and moors of northern Scotland. It has of recent years been discovered in northern England; perhaps this is proof that the weather is getting worse.

I do not think botanists will be popular for calling the Lady of the Woods warty, hairy or even dwarf, though the Latin names are pretty. Anyway, two species flourish abundantly in most parts of the kingdom, with only a slight emphasis in favour of the hairy birch in the wetter North and West, and the warty birch in the drier South and East. In northern Ireland however the hairy one is much more common than its sisten

41

*birchwood on Berkhamstead Common, merging into oakwood beyond*

**Silver or warty birch**
Twigs and buds hairless frequently pendulous
Bark white, but brown on young trees. Later often black at base of trunk
Leaves sharply pointed

**Common or hairy birch**
Twigs and buds usually hairy less often pendulous
Bark white on young trees not usually brown, nor black at the base when older
Leaves pointed but not sharply

**Dwarf birch**
Low shrub
Leaves round and blunt-toothed, distinctly veined below

*birches begin the transformation of an old slag-heap into woodland. Wigan, Lancashire*

In winter the ends of the twigs can be seen to be thickened by stiff catkins: these are male. As the leaves begin to open the catkins lengthen and hang, ready to scatter their pollen in the wind to the females, which are smaller and upright. The fruiting catkins in their turn mature and become pendulous and fat, until they disintegrate in September, releasing the tiny winged seeds.

In parts of Scotland, birch, pine and oak are the only local trees, with a scattering of rowan and holly. Here the birch was used for practically every need from smoking herrings, through furniture and small tools, to (using the bark) tanning and insulation. It was burnt for ordinary fuel, and made into charcoal for iron smelting. Brooms are still made of the twigs, and until plastic took over, cotton reels were turned from it. 'The birch' was of course much used for punishment, when punishment was no crime, and is now recommended by sex manuals for stimulation, if needed.

**Pioneer of pit-tips**

'Bring back the birch', declaims a modern 'concrete' poet in a poem consisting of just those words painted on a notice. He need not worry, the birch needs no assistance. The picture above shows a slag-heap, or more technically, a pit-tip, which has been left alone for perhaps 30 years. It speaks for itself. Pit-tips are of course dangerous lumps of grey desert when large and shaly, but they need not all be guiltily flattened and turned into parks. Especially the smaller older ones: they made wonderful dirt tracks for daring cyclists when I was little, and they doubled up as unexplored mountain ranges with yellow 'gold' for the digging. Eventually, the birches will grow, adding new patches of wild wood to our tidy country, so that small boys need not be vandals.

43

*bunching of small twigs may be caused by a fungus, a virus or a gall-mite, and affects other trees besides the birch. These harmless growths are called witches' brooms*

The family Betulacea consists of trees and shrubs and besides the birch includes the alder. Closely related are hornbeam and hazel. All these have single leaves alternately on the twig, and bear catkins.

The name, birch, comes straight from Old English, as befits a native tree. Names containing 'birk' are scattered everywhere. The Welsh *bedw* means birch (but not *bettws*; that is a chapel).

The toadstool of the pixies, red with light spots, is the fly agaric which grows in birchwoods and pinewoods. It has been used in many religions for inducing a state of trance, with luck; or stupor, on an off-day. The fungi are dried in the sun and are swallowed whole. The narcotic effect takes two hours to come on. To take more than one can be dangerous, but not, I am told, usually fatal.

*the dwarf birch,* Betula nana, *growing amongst the heather*

*boxwood near Aylesbury*

# BOXWOODS

There are only two or three boxwoods in Britain and parts of them are merely scrub, so the tree-botanists tend to ignore this beautiful evergreen. But scarcity adds value, and the trees grow to 20 feet, which is nearly their normal height in warmer climates. Box Hill in Surrey and a hillside in the Chilterns are the two remaining natural sites. A wood at Boxley, near Maidstone, is there no longer. Other place names beginning Box and Bux abound, at least some of them indicating the old sites of woods. A wood at Boxwell, in Gloucestershire, is reported, but this one is less likely to be natural in origin – it hardly matters as long as the trees grow wild.

The illustrations will show the nature of this tree, *Buxus sempervirens*, so beautifully wrought in all its detail. The leaves are formed like a shell or carapace and are pale underneath. Box loves shade and it grows on almost

*below : flowers in May and, right : the horned seed-capsules of box*

pure chalk, on north-facing hillsides, or in the shade of larger trees such as beeches. Scrub of box, which spreads on similar slopes, is thick and almost impassable, but interspersed, on the Chiltern site, with spurge laurel. Some beech and wych elm extend from nearby woods. There is little grass – a few stalks. Exposed to direct sun the leaves of the box have an unhealthy orange cast.

**Wood-engraving**

Boxwood is yellow, close-grained and heavy – it is said to sink in water. The boxwoods near London became immensely valuable around 1830–40, for the wood was used for engraving illustrations to periodicals like the *Penny Magazine* and the *Illustrated London News*, which were printed on the new steam presses. Copper engravings, which had been the fashion, could not be printed alongside type on the machines. Wood-engraving, that is cutting the endgrain to print, had been revived by the famous Thomas Bewick, who was also a naturalist. One of his blocks, the headpiece of the *Newcastle Courant*, was said to have printed a million copies.

Until the 1890's, when photo-engraving on metal became general, tons of boxwood blocks were used in printing. Endgrain boxwood, even imported from Turkey, cannot be got in large sizes – eight inches square is unusual. Large illustrations would be produced, often overnight, by several craftsmen whose work was joined imperceptibly to make one block. The trade in boxwood reached many thousands of pounds a year in London. Trees were so expensive that they were sold bit by bit. It is only surprising that any boxwoods remain, for the trade must have dwindled gradually and there would be no incentive to replant. The illustration overleaf, of hazelnuts, was photographed from a wood engraving printed in 1842. The name *Buxus* means flute, and box was used from ancient times for instruments both musical and mathematical. Up to the age of steel it made small wheels and pins, screws, shuttles, buttons and – nutcrackers. Boxwood turners' chips were used by herbalists as the basis of 'hysteric ale', also containing iron filings and a variety of innocuous herbs. It was recommended to be 'taken constantly by vapourous women'.

*box scrub on almost bare chalk*

*Male catkins and female flower which open at different times on the same twig*

# HAZEL

Though it is rarely tall enough to be properly called a tree, the hazel must be included in any study of woodland. Its shape is somewhat sprawling, but it is not entirely shrublike: it is a small tree. If left alone, which it very rarely is, it grows with a single distinct trunk. It certainly once did form extensive, pure hazelwoods. Historians refer to these as hazel *scrub*, without, as far as I can see, any justification apart from the present lowly stature of hazels, which shelter in the rocky valleys of hill country, or are coppiced, or grow in the shade of woods.

As birches followed the receding ice of the last glaciation of Europe, so hazel followed the birch. Since much of the birch, which has left its pollen from six to thirty feet under the ground, must have been the dwarf, *Betula nana,* no more than two feet high, it is clear that the hazel must have been the first actual tree to cover some of the English and Irish plains, as they gradually ceased to be tundra. This is a large claim, but the historians admit that on some Irish sites, '…the total of hazel pollen reaches up to seventeen times the total of other tree pollens, and up to four times…in England' (Winifred Pennington, *The History of British Vegetation*, 1969). Taller trees, particularly pine, wych elm, oak and lime, took their places over a period of two thousand years and hazel ceased to be dominant. But it persisted as the main shrub of the forest. It is now commonly found here in damp oakwoods – and, we are told, in pinewoods on a Baltic island. In some parts of Ireland hazel seems to have persisted as the main tree until cleared in Tudor times. A rich and beautiful hazelwood fills a remote valley in the Burren hills of County Clare, and prostrate 'wind-cut' trees creep over the more sheltered rocks, fruiting vigorously in that fantastic, grey landscape. Natural hazel-woods are to be found in the Lake District and in western Scotland; but it is not a mountain tree.

It is an interesting thought that in most of Britain, in the Boreal period, some six thousand years before Christ, the ground must have been thickly covered with perfectly edible nuts. How did the trees get here? It

47

must be remembered that Britain was part of the rapidly warming land mass of Europe, where hazel was also common. It has been shown to have been a staple food of Stone Age man, who was in constant movement northwards. Nuts could float down the Rhine, and the Seine, which also flows north. Nuthatches will carry the seeds some way to crack them. Squirrels, of course store them, and beavers (now extinct here) store whole branches. Pigs would, no doubt, swallow some soft nuts whole – and so on.

Once hazel is established it will spread both by seeds and suckers. In the absence of competition from the taller warmth-loving trees it would shade out many low plants, including the dwarf birch. The hazel's typical field flora is early flowering – primroses and wood-anemones – while tree seedlings would make slow progress under its broad leaves, which remain until December. There is no reason to suppose that in post-glacial Britain hazel behaved as it does in modern coppices.

Hazel flowers very early in the year. Its male catkins are the 'lambs' tails' you see in the woods and hedges when everything else is bare. The female flower consists of a crimson pistil emerging from what appears to be a leaf bud, but is in fact a scaly catkin. The nuts, at first blond-green and downy, form within elegant sheaths (bracts or bracteoles) in groups of four. Twigs and leaves are hairy. The bark of the young trunk is brownish grey, smooth, and polished where exposed to the wind.

This is the only British wild tree which produces edible nuts. To plant a hazel you should keep the nuts fairly moist in sand until early spring; plant them six inches deep. The growing tree should be cut out in the centre to form a bowl shape for the best crop of nuts. It will tolerate shade and stony, dank soil, but needs plenty of sun to fruit well.

Large nuts from special strains of the common hazel, *Corylus avellana*, are called cobnuts. A distinct Mediterranean species, *C. maxima*, has bearded nuts called filberts. Kentish cobs, which appear in the English markets, are filberts or a hybrid. Since we also import thousands of tons of hazelnuts, planting in our gardens seems a good idea, in spite of all those old neglected coppices.

*left : early Victorian wood-engraving of filberts. Right : wild hazel nuts*

old hazel coppice,
Hatfield Forest, Essex

*(Map labels:)* Elman's Green · Street Coppice · Hampton's Coppice · Eight Wantz Ways · Takeley Hill · Middle Hollows · Elgin Coppice · Beggars Hill Coppice · Thurley's Straight · London Bridge · Round Coppice · London Road · The Warren · America · Gravelpit Coppice · Lodge Coppice · Lodge · Cottrel Ride · Collin's Coppice · Emblem's Coppice · Hall

## Coppices

Hazel was the original coppice tree. As we have seen, the forests when men first settled in Britain were full of hazel, or in places consisted entirely of it. New Stone Age men were builders and farmers, though semi-nomadic. They certainly must have used hazel for fences and houses. The first proof of regular coppicing comes from a Somerset causeway of the Bronze Age – some two thousand years later. This was made of ten foot poles, straight and of even diameter, which could only be produced from coppice, that is, trees growing close together and regularly cut to the ground.

The rise in sheep farming to a peak in Medieval England meant that more and more coppice wood was needed for fencing – essential in a countryside not enclosed by walls and hedges, (and mercifully free of barbed wire). The supply of natural hazel ran out and new groves were planted, their cutting carefully regulated. Coppice wood was much used in building, especially in wattle-and-daub areas (where there was no stone or brick), and coppices often included tall oaks, for beams. This gave a

49

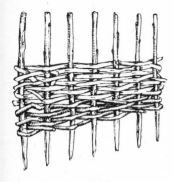

*hazel hurdle, half completed*

recognisable pattern, boringly referred to by foresters as coppice-with-standards – a sort of rooted timber yard.

Seven to ten years produces the right poles for splitting and making into wattles or hurdles, which are woven in the clearings out of the green wood, skillfully twisted and secured without ties or nails. Two or three acres would keep one man busy for a whole year and the coppice he worked would therefore be seven to ten times that, cut in rotation. Coppices provided a steady and reliable source of income to their owners; most old coppices survived into the age of wire and sawn imported timber because of the landowners' habit of breeding pheasants for shooting. Parts of old forests still bear the geometric patterns of coppices, now very much overgrown. They are hard to remove. H.L.Edlin, who is the source of my information, strikes a gloomy note: '...the hazel gives no quarter and it is simpler and often cheaper to cut it all flat and replant the ground with a smother-crop of some fast growing conifer such as Japanese larch or Douglas fir '.

Thin hazel wood from the coppices – and indeed from any odd tree – had other uses besides fencing and wattle-and-daub. The thatcher uses it for spars; fishing rods used to be made from it, also riding switches and bird-traps. Hop poles were, and bean poles still can be, cut from the coppice. The waste from the coppices would fire bread-ovens – and provided bits of wood for a thousand purposes we have forgotten.

Water diviners use hazel rods or forked sticks to add mystery to their craft, which is, no doubt, half instinct and half informed observation. In even more credulous times, people 'divined' metal and treasure, and criminals. The hazel was, according to the Irish Druids, the tree of wisdom; its nut the food of knowledge. Perhaps it *was* the staple food of their forefathers.

*hazel tree in a Highland valley*

# HOLLY

*above : hedgerow hollies which have survived the removal of the hedge*

Our commonest native evergreen, except for the ever-present ivy, holly has only reached its present wide distribution in comparatively recent times. It was, as it is now, a shrub of oakwoods and beechwoods, where it grows thinly but persistently in the shade. When a gap appears in the forest canopy, and at the edges of woods, it can grow strongly, and will flower and fruit in abundance. This is where the story of its present prevalence begins, for at first the woods which were warm enough for this plant of the Atlantic climates – had no edges. It was only when forest clearance began that holly began to spread strongly. It is of course naturally armoured against vegetarian animals. So specialised is the armour that it rarely extends beyond the height that can be reached by cows or deer: the leaves are nearly always spiny below six or eight feet, and quite entire at the top of the tree.

Holly gained a further lease of life when the country was enclosed in hedges. There are some very old hedges of pure holly, but the normal field hedge of hawthorn offers a protected seeding ground frequented by birds which eat both kinds of berry. Hedgers, whose job it was to cut and lay the bushes – to keep them full at the bottom – would leave certain trees to grow: the ashes and oaks, out of respect for them as trees and because they do not lend themselves to laying: the elms, for the same reasons and also because they had usually been planted there: the holly because it was holy – or would make good fuel if, next winter, you were too cold to be religious.

Holly produces instant fuel, like the ash. Even the leaves burn fiercely,

*the pink flower buds open into four petals*

and the logs flame beautifully, though it must be admitted that the heat is soon gone. 'The Holly and the Ivy' in the old carol, refer to the Holly Boy and the Ivy Girl, who were some sort of pagan survival at Shrove Tuesday junketings. Both holly and hawthorn have been designated as the thorn which made Christ's derisive crown. But in older memories the hawthorn was a pagan tree of fertility festivals in May, while holly, before we imported Norwegian Christmas trees, was the original Christmas tree. The custom survives as you know, of ripping out the berried branches, or all that can be reached, and sticking them around the house to wither. The berries symbolise the drops of Christ's blood: inappropriate, I would say, to celebrate His birth.

In spite of this, holly seems still to increase. It is popular for the hedges of town gardens and parks, where its leaves, which stay on the tree for three years (not for ever) collect a lot of grime. But even though our woods shrink and our hedges are demolished, holly berries will still be there in the tops of town trees to be carried by birds to all parts of the agricultural countryside. And superstition, or sentiment, still preserves hollies – as the heading picture shows.

Holly prefers the damper side of Britain and is sensitive to persistent frost of as little as minus one degree centigrade. Struggling small trees can be found in river valleys of western Scotland, where it seems to stand some chance against the sheep and deer.

**A holly wood**

It forms a classic 'shrub layer' in oakwoods, especially in those natural oakwoods of screes and rocks, where the holly will often extend beyond the limit of the oaks and form woods of its own. Such a wood lies by the Upper Lake of Killarney, between the oakwoods of the roughly terraced mountainside and the raised bog beside the lake. Here holly is the major element in a distinctive and beautiful environment. The wood is full of strange atmosphere. As in so many natural places which people have left alone, one feels a sense of design, as if in a garden remarkable for the restraint and luxury of its colours and forms. The floor, here smooth, here

*wrinkled and warted skin-like bark of an old holly in County Kerry*

*right : holly leaves in a beechwood*

broken by lines of scattered boulders, is entirely in the rich velvet green of a number of mosses, which cover every stone and the trunks of all the trees, some of which are heavily twisted with ivy. The branches of the oaks carry ferns and are sometimes heavily incrusted with lichens. The stems and branches of the hollies are almost pure white, not the dingy pewter of the urban tree. Their shapes are contorted into every conceivable variation of the upright branching form normally associated with trees. Some appear to gesticulate tragically, while others take on the monumental stance and forms of sculpture. The scars of branches casually lopped or accidentally broken are surrounded by grotesque swellings, as if the bark had been molten, while branches and even trunks which have crossed and touched are fused and welded into unexpected patterns.

The clean bark of the hollies is etched and minutely wrinkled and folded into parallel and radial patterns and is covered in places with spherical warts. Mosses grow in the angles of branches which catch the rainwater. The clear silvery white of the holly bark is reflected in the white lichens which cover any stone not wholly encased in moss. Through the wood flows a clear dark stream, sometimes muttering under hollow rocks, then splashing into pools made by fallen trees which have dammed its flow.

There are few other plants in the wood: foxgloves in clear places, and bracken. Wood sorrel, looking more than usually delicate, grows out of the moss. Caves are masked with luxuriant ferns: outcrops of the bedrock are covered with heather. In the upper part of the wood one is hardly conscious of the oaks overhead. Farther down there are no oaks and the shade of the hollies is open enough for grass and primroses. The stream flows out through tufted grassy bog, then winds in a natural meadow to the lake. The side of the wood gives way sharply, over a ridge, to rocks and heather, and then to the turf of the bog, with a few birches on the drained edge.

The vigorous growth of the holly in and outside the Killarney oakwoods is due to the moist climate and the protection given by the mountains from winds and frost. Alongside the holly, rhododendron thrives, not merely pushing out suckers but springing from seed. The strawberry tree, *Arbutus unedo*, grows here on rocky ledges and nowhere else in Britain. Still, this climate is only a slightly intensified version of that enjoyed by much of western Britain, and the perfection and richness of these surroundings could be reflected in many other associations of species, *provided they are left alone*.

The holly, *Ilex aquifolium*, is usually either a male or female tree. Flowers of both sexes are first pink buds and later cruciform (of course), the female having a large ovary between false stamens. The flowers are short-lived, appearing in mid or late May, and pollinated by insects, particularly bees. Each berry contains several seeds.

A variety called hedgehog-holly has leaves with a lot of spines, and there are cultivated varieties, some with hideous yellow leaves.

*holly wood with grassy floor and primroses*

*trunk of an English oak
with typical shrub and
commonest bird*

# OAKS AND OAKWOODS

There are 450 species of oak in the temperate parts of the Northern
Hemisphere, plus a few hybrids. Many can be found in Kew Gardens – or at
least, I collected 52 different oak leaves there, one autumn. What we call the
common or English oak, *Quercus robur*, (or *Q. pedunculata*), grows all over
Europe and Asia, but in Britain has a distinctly imperialist image. 'Heart of
oak are our ships', etc. dates from the eighteenth century. Earlier, in 1662,
John Evelyn embarked on his classic, *Silva, or a Discourse of Forest Trees*, to
prevent 'the sensible and notorious decay of our Wooden Walls'.
Evelyn recommended that 'His Majesty's forests and chases be stored with
this spreading tree at handsome intervals, by which grazing might be
improved for the feeding of deer and cattle under them, benignly visited
with the gleams of the sun, and adorned with the distant landscapes
appearing through the glades and frequent valleys; nothing could be more
ravishing. We might also sprinkle fruit-trees amongst them for cider...'
    Only 200 mature trees were left of the old Forest of Dean when it was
surveyed in 1667, and Evelyn's advice was heeded, except perhaps for the
fruit trees for cider. An open pattern of replanted forest was established,
and echoed in many a park. Some land was enclosed for plantations.
    The demand for oak timber continued. In 1812 it was stated in a
parliamentary report that no less than two thousand well-grown oak trees
were used in the building of one 74-gun ship. Thousands of acres of the
New Forest were enclosed for planting oaks and here many old trees have
survived the age of wooden ships.

55

*roadside oak tree in winter*

Large old trees with spreading, angular branches were especially valued by the ship-builders for their 'knees and crucks'. Timber, before the days of power saws, was shaped with the adze along the lines of its growth, at least for large members forming the hulls of ships and the roofs of buildings. Trees of the right shape and size had to be searched out in the woods, and they were bought as standing trees, gradually increasing many times in value as they were sawn and transported to the docks or building sites. Large trees were not so much felled as dismembered; the great branches sawn off and lowered by tackle and even the trunk bisected as it stood. A tree in Monmouthshire took, 'Five men twenty days stripping and cutting down...two sawyers were five months converting it, Sundays excepted'. This tree was over 400 years old. In 1810, 'the bark alone fetched £200, and the tree when sawn, £675, though the owner only had £100, because it was sold as a standing tree thought to be unsound.'

Oak bark was used by tanners. The whole tree is rich in tannic acid. The leather industry was also supplied from coppices all over the country which were regularly stripped of their bark. The old used bark was often spread on the streets near a house where someone was ill, to deaden the sound of the horses' shoes and the rumbling of carriage wheels.

**Most durable timber**  Our old oak trees tend to be picturesque rather than useful and as H.L.Edlin points out: 'we have little good mature close-grown high forest, and hardly any of this of natural origin. The few good stands that have survived the wars were mostly planted by early nineteenth century landowners'. With oak trees, as you see, we are in a world of economics, where the users of one century suffer from the habits of the previous two. But the timber of the Common Oak, whether English or not, remains the most durable and strongest. More or less modern applications are docks and lock gates, boats, chassis of heavy vehicles, the beds of heavy machinery, and railway sleepers. In smaller sections, but its strength still important, are the

*oakwood in the wild near the Upper Lakes of Killarney, April*

arms of telegraph poles, ladder rungs, wine barrels, flooring, panelling and furniture. It is also very good fuel, and we can suppose that most of our native forests went up in smoke.

But the use of trees, though sometimes excessive, has not necessarily ever been the first cause of reducing the woods. Grazing and clearance for agriculture are the real cause of woodland decay. Of course, exploitation of the trees went hand-in-hand with clearance, but where there was a known demand, such as for charcoal in the ironworks of Sussex, or even for 'coals' in the gentry's houses, steps were taken to ensure the future supply, either by organised coppicing, which left the trees to grow again, or by merely lopping above the height of grazing animals (which at least lengthens the life of the tree). The result was the perpetuation of some woodlands, not their destruction.

**Common rights**

Oaks were valued for their acorns or mast. Rights of common pannage or mast existed from early feudal times until the enclosures in the late eighteenth century, and still continue in the New Forest. In the Domesday Book many landlords returned estimates of their woodlands and wastelands expressed in terms of the number of swine they would feed. Other common rights allowed villagers to remove wood for repairing farm implements, 'ploughbote', and hedges, 'haybote', and for building and fuel. Dead wood could also be removed from the trees by hook and crook. The right to feed swine was the least destructive of trees (pasturage was the worst, and turbery, the right to cut peat, also killed seedlings). The swine were gathered under some particularly productive oaks (or beeches) and roughly fenced in for a day or two while the swineherd played on his horn. The beasts learnt to associate the music with the rich feed, and the herdsman could then

*branches of ancient
dwarfed oaks covered with
lichen, Dartmoor*

*right : sessile oak ; new
leaves*

control them in the open forest. For all the natural super-abundance of seed
that the swine removed, they trampled a few acorns into the ground, safe
from the wood-mice, and likely to germinate in the spring when the pigs
would be elsewhere (mostly eaten).

Oaks still account for one third of our hardwood trees, and this appears to
be a norm for the 60 centuries it has been established here. During this time
the native forest has shrunk to a scattered part of our seven per cent of trees
on the land. After the early post-glacial preponderance of birch, then pine,
and the enormous spread of hazel, the amounts of oak pollen deposited in
peat came to a peak in the wet Atlantic period. There must have been dense,
high, oak forest. The average frequency increases towards historical times,
while hazel, equally widespread, decreases from the massive totals of the
Boreal period to 60 per cent and less of the total pollen of other trees. (Hazel,
*Corylus,* pollen is treated separately by paleobotanists, partly because it
could be confused with that of bog-myrtle, and partly because hazel is
classed as a shrub.) The picture that emerges, to my very inexpert eye, is of
great oak forests spreading and thinning out, with other trees, over a country
much of which was under hazel trees. The hazel which started as a shrub
layer under the Boreal pines retreated again to its shrub status under the
oaks, after probably acting as nursery to them.

The oak which colonised Ireland and most of western and northern
Britain was *Quercus petrae*, or *Q. sessiliflora*, the durmast oak. Botanists are
careful to separate the two species, *Q. robur*, and *Q. petrae*, and their
habitats, but in England they are very much mingled and trees can be found
with variable characteristics of both. In Sherwood Forest, we are told, the

*oak plantation in a corner of what used to be Sherwood Forest*

separate species and their hybrid flourished in natural cohabitation. Below are the technical differences.

---

*Querqus robur (Q. pedunculata)*
**common oak**

Up to 80 or even 100 ft
Twigs hairless

Leaves four inches long, deeply lobed with auricles at the base, on short stalks.

Acorns on stalks.

Deeper, heavier soils and clay.

Tends to S.E. but planted everywhere and naturalised

*Q. petrae (Q. sessiliflora)*
**durmast or sessile oak**

Up to 80 ft
Twigs downy

Leaves five inches long, less deeply lobed, tapering at base, on long stalks ($\frac{1}{2}$ to 1 inch)

Acorns clustered close to twig

Shallower, more acid soils and sands

Tends to westerly oceanic climate or hills

---

More pedunculate oak has been planted than sessile, and few of the oakwoods have been allowed to regenerate naturally. But they have often been cleared and planted repeatedly on ancient sites.

59

**Plants of oakwoods**

Apart from the old habit of planting or thinning the trees to allow them to spread out (and often filling the spaces with coppice), the natural shade of oakwoods is not dense. The oaks are often, but not always, mixed with other trees, according to the type of soil and position. Ash and elm, maple (or more commonly sycamore), cherries, birches, hornbeam, poplars and alder: all can compete on different soils in open oakwoods. The shrub layer is equally rich and varied, from the healthy holly trees of the humid, western oakwoods, through hazel, to hawthorn and elder which are common in the small scattered woods of today. Almost every shrub can be found in oakwood, including the sallows, while the field layer can contain every woodland plant, including meadow grass.

I find it impossible to suggest what is most typical. Britain is remarkable for the variety of its terrain, and there are noted oakwoods in every English

*oak flowers and fruits,*
*English hybrid species*

and Welsh county (with a slight shortage in Pembrokeshire), and in most of the counties of Scotland and Ireland. Perhaps the most distinctive patterns are those of old forests with great trees, bracken, and wandering herds of deer, or the closer, more silent woods, with bluebells in spring. But dog's mercury and brambles, neither very poetic, are just as common. For ancient oakwooks in virtually their natural state, you must visit Dartmoor or County Kerry, and be prepared for some very rough walking. Oaks growing near their limit of altitude or exposure will be stunted, even though thick and very old. In mild wet climates the trees are heavily clad in mosses and lichens, and bear other trees on their branches – rowans – or plants like bilberry, grasses and wood sorrel. Ferns, particularly common polypody, sprout from the mosses and from damp junctions of branch and trunk. Everything that grows on the rocky floor of these woods, also grows in the trees, producing a quite disturbing effect of fairyland. Near the Dartmoor wood the dreamy atmosphere is a little spoilt by sheep dying of broken legs, reminding us that such ancient woodland survives only because it is rooted in heaps of boulders.

Old woods of scrubby or stunted oaks, especially in the north and in

*very old stunted oak on Dartmoor*

Scotland, often owe their low stature to random coppicing and lopping, as well as to exposure.

About 300 different insects and small animals make use of the oak, its leaf, buds, flower, fruit, bark, wood and root. Other insects feed on them or on the many lichens and fungi which depend on oakwood, live or dead. Blue-tits and other tits, robins, hedge-sparrows, tree-creepers and other small birds hunt in the branches. Squirrels, with dormice and jays, feed on and store the acorns: wood mice, rooks, nuthatches, pheasants and wood

*scrub oak, Isle of Skye*

| mosses covering trunk of oak and ivy stem | oak marble gall | lung lichen on branch |
|---|---|---|
| | artichoke galls of oak buds | mildew on leaves of sapling |
| polypody ferns growing in moss on oak limb | oak cherries on leaves | burr on trunk |

epihytes, insect galls
and parasites, none of
which seriously impedes
the growth of the tree.
The burr on the trunk was
probably caused by careless
cropping. But burr-oak was
valuable timber

pigeons eat them. Shrews populate the leaf litter, always busy, much of their food fattened on oak leaf before reaching the ground. Owls quarter the wood for their prey. Botanists, zoologists and biologists compile statistics.

**Oak eaters**

Here are some oak tree inhabitants:

Galls, which employ the vegetable growth of the trees, are caused by some midges: their larvae fold the leaves

by gall wasps: *oak apples* – of irregular round shape contain several larvae and often other insects

*oak marbles* – These are the very common galls once imported for making ink (the galls are simply bottled in water). Part of the life cycle of this wasp continues in different, small galls in the tops of Turkey oaks

*oak artichokes* – deformed buds. The female when hatched lays eggs in the flowers, producing other hairy galls there

*oak cherries* – Unusual round galls on the leaves

*leaf spangles* – of various kinds are caused by different gall wasps. Other gall wasps feed in the roots of the tree.

*spangle galls*

Oak leaves are eaten by the leaf mining larvae of weevils, sawflies and some micro moths. Leaf miners make blister mines and galleries in the leaves. Leaf rollers are caterpillars of the green tortrix moth. Other micro moths make webs in the leaves without rolling them.

Many larger moths feed on oak leaves, among them several Geometers or loopers, of which the angular caterpillars of the winter moth and the mottled umber are characteristic. They have wingless females which also climb up orchard trees. Pupae either hang in the tree or descend on threads to be protected by dead leaves. Other oak-feeding Geometers are the spring usher, the emerald moths common and blotched, the maiden's blush, the willow beauty, the false mocha and the August thorn. Cockchafers, or Maybugs, can swarm and defoliate a whole tree, causing it to produce a second crop of leaves. Their larvae feed mainly on grass and cereal roots. Perhaps because of efficient farming, Maybugs are less common than they were.

Aphids, fast breeding and multitudinous, drink from leaf sap, leaving yellow patches. There is a special oak-aphid, *Phyloxera quercus*. Lacewings, ladybirds and ants, as well as birds, feed on the aphids – fortunately or there would be no woods.

Other plant-bugs, the capsids, drink some sap from the twigs but they are mainly carnivorous. Among them is the impressively named, *Dryophilocoris flaviquadrimaculatus*.

Bark beetles (Scolytidae) including ambrosia beetles, create patterned galleries under the bark and introduce their choice of fungi (which sometimes grows too well and stifles them). The elm-bark beetles also attack the oak, less destructively, while *Scolytus intricatus* is named the oak-bark beetle. Stag beetles breed on rotting stumps.

Other beetles bore into the wood, not the leaves; the goat moth, whose caterpillar is supposed to smell like a goat, feeds on rotting stumps, not peculiarly the oak's. The oak eggar moth does not lay eggs on oaks but is named from the colours of its wings.

*Lucombe oak in Cambridge, December. This semi-evergreen is a cross between the cork oak and the Turkey oak*

*leaves of black oak, a decorative tree of American origin*

*acorns of a Japanese evergreen oak, Kew Gardens*

*acorn of Turkey oak. This tree is a native of Southern Europe and Asia frequently planted in Britain*

*trunk of holm oak, Oxfordshire. This is the commonest evergreen oak grown in Britain*

The Celtic *derry* means oakwood and the name, Druid, is supposed to have the same root. But the sparse Celtic imagery contains nothing of oaks. The oak, and the mistletoe which now very rarely grows on it, were *perhaps* included in some way in Druidical rites. The Yule Log, perhaps deriving from the Druids' sacred fire, was traditionally of oak – though naturally enough, since it is common and gives the best heat. Whether the Druids chose to worship in groves of trees or were driven there by the Romans is not clear. It would seem strange that people should make their commonest tree sacred. Perhaps great oaks were left in ancient clearings as meeting places – as they were for centuries afterwards.

The list of old oaks with names is a long one. There are still many grotesque and swollen ruins with at least 500 years of history, standing about the country, bound and supported by iron stays and crutches. They were landmarks when the only others were hills and church towers.

The original Royal Oak sheltered the prince who became Charles II – in Shropshire, while Cromwell's troops were searching for him. 'A great oak that had been lopped some three or four years before, and being grown out again, very bushy and thick, could not be seen through; and here we laid all the day.' The tree was later dismembered by souvenir hunters, some of whom took only some acorns to plant new Royal Oaks. Many other old trees are associated with historical and legendary concealments, rebellions, hangings and trysts.

Oaks, as well as other large trees, marked boundaries. Others served as pulpits, or had the gospels read under them at the corners of parishes (Gospel Oak is an underground station in north London), or were the scenes of fairs and festivals. Oaks and 'oaken shaws' are preserved in dozens of place-names, also in some beginning with the Old English 'ac'.

The oak has always a benevolent image and its practical virtues once extended beyond the use of its wood. All parts of it were used in medicine as 'proper in diarrhoea, dysentary and all other excessive evacuations. The bark and leaves in decoctions are very useful in spitting of blood, profuse menses, floodings, bleeding piles, Fluor Albus etc. Acorns appease the cholic, given in powder, from half a drachm to a drachm, in milk broth.' So wrote the herbalist in 1800. Let Sir John Evelyn have the last word: 'It is reported that the very shade of this tree is wholesome, that sleeping or lying under it becomes a present remedy to paralytics'.

*leaf-litter, New Year's Day*

# SCOTS PINE

*above : natural pinewood below Ben Eighe*

This is our native pine tree and our only conifer if you exclude the yew and juniper, which have fleshy, not woody, cones. The Scots pine is a source of good timber – usually called red deal – and has ranked second in economic importance to oak, though I suppose it will take second place to spruce, as the great plantations mature. The great Caledonian forest, or what remains of it, is part of a much greater northern European forest of this tree, *Pinus sylvestris*, of which the Scots pine is a local, very hardy form. The tree is variable – the leaves alone can be from one to four inches, and seeds from different countries have been used in replanting, so increasing its variability in Britain.

Pines germinate easily and grow on a wide range of poor soils from wet to dry, but do not compete with the spread of tall deciduous trees. Pine burns easily and does not coppice, so once removed it is unlikely to return unless planted. Remains of large forests are buried in peat all over Britain. Heavy pollen deposits are found, as well as stumps at various levels and from the Irish bogs to the tops of the Pennines or the peat of the Fens. On some coasts pine roots are revealed by the tides as submerged forests.

The pine is often called a fir, quite reasonably as that is its name in most other languages. It will be useful here to distinguish between some common members of the family, Pinaceae, which are all trees with needle-shaped (or scaly) leaves and with, usually, woody cones. The timber is called softwood and is often resinous. All these trees are grown for their timber, except for the cedars, which are usually well established decorative trees.

*Abies:* **silver firs**
Needles alternate with white stripes below, usually in rows. Cones erect

*Cedrus:* **cedars**
Needles spirally to tufted, broad erect cones. Old trees have spreading planes

*Picea:* **spruces**
Needles mostly sharp on short pegs. Pointed trees, cones hanging

*Pseudostuga:* **Douglas firs**
Short needles irregularly arranged. Sharp, long, winter buds. Distinctive hanging cone with three-pointed bracts on scales

*Pinus:* **pines**
Needles in bundles of two to five according to species. Cones egg-shaped or pointed with thickened scales.

*Larix:* **larches**
Deciduous needles tufted on older shoots. Persistent small cones

Other trees in the family have scaly leaves: two groups of cypresses and the similar arbor vitae; redwoods (*Sequoia*), rather feathery; Wellingtonia (*Sequoiadendron*). *Metasequoia*, a recently discovered 'fossil' tree, and 'hemlock' (*Tsuga*), have blunt needles. Juniper and yew are dealt with separately. Some pictures of planted conifers will be found in chapter 7.

Pine followed closely on the period of maximum birchwoods which occurred early in the post-glacial period. Pine and hazel were dominant at times but everywhere, except in Scotland, and East Anglia, gave way to oak, alder and elm as the climate softened. Where soils were too sandy or peaty for deciduous woods some pine remained while over most of the country the woods began to be undermined by the soggy sphagnum mosses. The climate became drier and the bogs dried out a little so that pines as well

*male catkins and right, pine leaves and cone*

*trunks of pines near Balmoral Castle. The orange tint of the bark distinguishes the native Scots pine from other pines*

as other trees recovered their ground. The dramatic process I have just 'sketched in' took 8,000 years and occurred in varying patterns in different parts of the peninsula, which during this time became the British Isles. Both birch and pine, as well as hazel when *not* shaded, produce very ample pollen which can carry for long distances, so our picture may well be distorted. Also pines and peat are often neighbours, and the general opinion of phytogeographers is that in southern Britain pine did not attain the dominance of birch, nor the persistence of oak.

Still, pinewoods remained in historical times as we guess from references to pines or 'fyrres' in various English counties, north and south. The process of clearance and exploitation removed them and regeneration was impossible until the seventeenth- and eighteenth-century landowners began to plant their parks. Odd groups of pines in the countryside are likely to have spread from their use of this conifer to nurse other trees and, occasionally, on the tops of hills, to catch the eye. Pines have also been planted as windbreaks. On heaths and old commons in Sussex and Surrey they spread, and give their character to countryside familiar to Pooh bear, and beautifully drawn by E.H. Shepard. On Breckland heaths, once given over to rabbits, the Forestry Commission has planted pines which now spread outside the plantations. The great Caledonian forest, once covering all but the mountain tops of Scotland, consisted entirely of pines, with oak below and birch above – and juniper. The timber line is now mostly well below 2,000 feet but is said to have been up to 2,500 feet.

Everywhere in Scotland the pinewoods were destroyed from Stuart times onwards. They were a supposedly inexhaustible supply of timber, which was floated away down lochs and rivers, having been sold for as little as sixpence a tree. Sheep became the major source of wealth, though not for clansmen or crofters. To quote Doctor Hobsbaum: 'The highlands became what they have ever since remained, a beautiful desert. When sheep farming declined the rich sports of stalking deer and shooting grouse provided a quicker profit than planting trees. The heavily stocked deer had the same effect as sheep, while regular burning, to provide new heather for the grouse, demolished any seedlings not eaten. On loch islands and in other protected places, the pines return and enrich the ground.

**Scottish scenery**

The remaining tracts of forest are large enough to give some idea of native Scottish scenery. The best known are parts of Glen More (some of it recently devastated by a fire); the adjoining Cairngorm Nature Reserve, including Rothiemurchus Forest; the Black Wood of Rannoch, Glen Affric Forest (59,000 acres) Inverness, and Ballochbuie Forest, part of Balmoral. There are others, smaller, very attractive, and carfeully conserved. Heather, bilberry and cowberry continue under the trees – the woods are usually loose and open, though Gilpin, an eighteenth-century writer, tells of 'compact bodies' of Scots pine, 'the heads drawn up . . . the stems becoming mere poles'. In closed woods like this there would be nothing on the floor except needles. Such probably were the woods that have gone – they were the best timber. Probably both pine and birch, growing in Scotland naturally, are scattered leavings from stands of good timber.

From a distance, the pines on a Scottish hillside are a good green, and have a soft rounded appearance that seems uncharacteristic of this rugged tree. In fact the young tree is conical, and older trees not devastated by wind form rounded crowns. The leaves of the native tree are short. It grows slowly and produces better timber than southern strains.

The male flowers are clusters of round catkins which produce, in May or June, clouds of yellow pollen. The bark forms irregular oblong plates, grey at the base into shining orange-brown further up. The leaves of the Scots pine grow in pairs from a short sheath – but so do the leaves of a dozen other species of pine. I think the best recognition feature is the bunchy texture of the foliage – once you know it you recognise it like a friend.

*seeds of pine*

# YEW

At Clacton-on-Sea, Essex, about 250,000 years ago someone left a spear made of yew which is the world's oldest known artefact of wood. Survival is the theme of this native conifer with poisonous leaves. The yew is closely associated with the monuments of men, from prehistoric sheltering groves to its hallowed position in modern churchyards. The first postglacial, (as distinct from interglacial) record came from county Cavan; and of several others early in the postglacial period, Dr Godwin says four are 'associated with the Neolithic Culture. Records of Bronze Age association are still more frequent and others occur along with Roman and Iron Age occupation layers'.

Yew woods are not common: apparently they never have been. The best known are at Kingley Vale, close to neolithic sites, near Chichester. The trees can be very old, as much as 1,000 years, though the oldest are really collections of relatively new trunks formed round the decayed original and even growing out of the top of it.

Yew trees protected men while they rested from hunting, or built nearby, or preached the Christian gospel: so they have been protected by men. It would not be surprising to be told that the sacred groves of the Druids were of yew. This is the only British tree to have kept its Celtic name, *Iw*. Its scientific name is *Taxus baccata*. The specific refers to the berries.

Animals avoid the foliage except for a few green shoots. As winter fodder it would be fatal. The berries consist of a single seed partly encased in

71

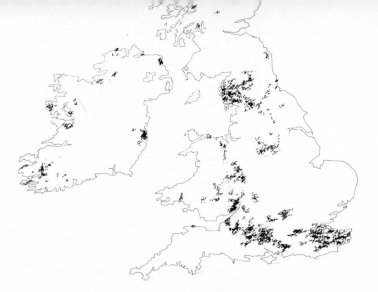

sweet, pink flesh. The seed and its hard shell are poisonous, but not the cup,
which is eaten by thrushes, who either avoid the seed or swallow it whole
without harm. The round yellow flowers form under the protection of the
leaves in early March, the male and female usually, but not invariably, on
separate trees. The female flowers are green and scaly – cone-like, at
least at this stage. The timber is brown, heavy and strong. Yew was used for
long-bows, but mostly it was imported from the European yew forests.
A late-medieval law insisted that every cask of wine shipped was to be
accompanied by six bow-staves.

All the native sites of yews are on well-drained calcareous soil and
protected from the harsher winds. Odd trees are to be found in beechwoods
on the chalk escarpments: they flourish in this shade, for their vegative
processes occur before and after the beeches are in leaf. There are some
yews in Gordale Scar, and scattered in other limestone areas of Yorkshire
and the southern part of the Lake District but not in Scotland, though there
was a Yew Tree Island (probably of planted trees) in Loch Lomond, from
which 300 trees were taken in the 1820's.

The best explanation for the planting of yews in churchyards (two in
Welsh ones), is that they were there before the churches. The foliage was
used to decorate the church at Easter, but this tradition most likely started
because the tree was handy. (Species for festive branches are always
interchangeable: sallow for Palm Sunday and birches for May, where there
was no palm or May blossom). Sprigs of yew were certainly cast into graves
and still are.

*'The old Yew-tree at Crom
Castle', Co. Fermanagh,
engraved in 1840*

*male flowers of yew, early April*

*yew berries or cones, December*

This sad tree bears patiently the shapes it is cut into, from 20 foot high walls to cocks and urns. A narrow shaped (fastigiate) variety is called Irish yew because it was first found in Fermanagh. It has leaves in a close radial pattern, a bit like juniper.

*sculptured Irish yews in a Somerset churchyard*

# 3 - OTHER TREES NATIVE AND NATURALISED

In the last chapter we established the six main native trees, all of which can grow in woods of a single species. Of the other four which were included, box and hazel are usually called shrubs; holly and yew are usually assumed not to form woods. But there are living examples to bear me out and these are important trees, both today and historically. It is of course anomalous to have included species like holm oak, but I think no one would want genera to be scattered over the book in separate species.

In each chapter I have used alphabetical order of common names. Of the trees which follow, it could be argued that some do form woods or have done in the past: wych-elm and the small-leaved lime, for instance. But these woods are gone. Most elms and limes in the landscape are incidental and derived from planted parents. The hawthorn can be said to be as much a tree as hazel or box and as likely to form woods, or at least thickets. This is so, but it is overwhelmingly a hedge or scrub tree – and hawthorn woods are uncomfortable places. Woods of sycamore are not unknown – in fact the sycamore is a special case; superbly adaptable, yet having made all its progress between Elizabeths I and II. Poplar woods are all planted, but there are small natural woods of aspen; and so on. No hard rule is intended, only convenient and moderately meaningful groups, as a means of knowing trees.

## CRAB APPLE AND WILD CHERRIES

The wild crab is a small bent tree of hedges and wild places. It is easily confused with wildings, escaped from orchards, or survivors of old orchard sites. Sometimes it is a wild form of cultivated crab. Like all apples it flowers on short spurs, which accumulate multiple scars, while the shoots simply grow. The leaves are rolled in the bud, not folded, and when they open are hairless, nearly hairless or hairy below, according to different authorities. The twigs carry spines sometimes, and sometimes do not. But the fruit is always hard and sour. Birds break up the apples and scatter the seeds nearby so that there are often young trees near a parent.

The blossom, white or pink, appears in early May with the opening leaves. Pollination is by insects, including honey bees.

Hadfield distinguishes a sweeter crab (with persisting down under the leaves), not native, but the ancestor of cultivated apples. This is surely correct, for eating-apples did not originate in England, where they were perfected, but in Paradise. They were guarded by a fearsome dragon in the Garden of the Hesperides.

But the little green apples of the crab tree are left lying on the ground, in spite of the excellence of crab apple jelly and crab apple wine. The juice or pulp without sugar was called verjuice, and used to cure sprains and scalds. With cream it made a syllabub. The tree produces small, hard timber.

*left : wild cherry or gean, Herts. Right : bird cherry on Dee-side, Braemar*

The large Rosacea family, which contains the apples and pears, also includes, under the generic name, *Prunus*, our two wild cherries. The blackthorn or sloe is also *Prunus*, as are the cultivated plums, apricots and almonds, and a common evergreen, the cherry laurel, which often runs wild.

The wild cherry, gean, or mazard, *P. avium*, can be a tall tree, and is frequent in beechwoods, where its shiny, reddish bark, strongly marked with horizontal lenticels and inclined to peel, is often all there is to identify it at ground level. The white flowers, on long stalks from persisting bud scales, are in typical cherryflower clusters, not so full as the flowering cherries of the streets and parks. The leaves and flowers come together, in May, and the leaves, inclined to droop on long stalks, also spring from a common base on the shoot. The fruits are said to be fairly sweet, mostly stone – but the birds get them before they are ripe.

There are double-flowered mazards in parks, these do not fruit. Other flowering cherries are usually of Japanese origin. The gean or mazard is one parent of the various delicious cherries that come from the orchards of Kent. Cherry wood was used in delicate pieces of furniture of the eighteenth and nineteenth centuries.

**The bird cherry**

The other wild cherry is the bird cherry, *P. padus*, usually a small tree with flowers that come in early June, after the leaves. The flowers are in long spikes, not clusters. The small trees usually grow along the sides of streams in the north, rarely in southern England. The fruit is even less edible than the gean's, but the flowers can be spectacular, especially with a backdrop of blue Scottish mountains.

Both the wild cherries have a fossil record beyond Roman times in Britain, but these are not very well documented. The bird cherry is common in Scandinavian postglacial deposits. It was mentioned, as a wild tree, and if we can trust the translation, by an Irish poet of the tenth century.

*chestnuts in summer*

# CHESTNUT

The wood of the sweet or Spanish chestnut is hard and durable, like that of the oak, but it splits easily. It is grown in southern England now for making chestnut palings – split triangular poles bound with wire for fences. The fruit ripens here but uncertainly. The chestnuts that are still roasted in London streets come from specialised strains which produce large nuts, in Italy or southern France. The French have trees called *marroniers*, distinguished from mere *châtaigniers*.

The Romans brought their native chestnuts to Britain: whether they planted trees we do not know. The peasants of northern Italy used chestnuts as a staple food where wheat did not grow easily. The trees grow in their mountains up to 2,500 feet. Flour, *pollenta*, made from chestnuts, can be

*chestnut coppice in west Sussex*

*male flowers, with female visible at base of leaf-stalk. Right: bark of an old tree at Hatfield House, Herts*

*section of chestnut paling*

made into cakes or fritters or into a sort of porridge, boiled in milk. Perhaps in these forms it was used by the Roman invaders. Pliny said the nuts were best roasted; they were sometimes ground to a meal, converted by the women into 'a wretched substitute for bread', eaten during religious fasts. To more ancient writers 'soft chestnuts' were a delicacy: but perhaps Virgil's '*castaneae molles*', were water-chestnuts?

Evelyn regretted that we gave them to swine. He wrote that the nut 'is a lusty and masculine food for rusticks at all times, and of better nourishment for husbandmen than cole and rusty bacon, yea, or beans to boot'. And: 'the bread of the flour is exceedingly nutritive; it is a robust food, and makes women well-complexioned, as I have read in a good author'. He had chestnut trees planted in Greenwich Park. Chestnuts flourished in southern England, especially in the sand of the Weald, and came to be regarded as native trees. A vague, but possibly true, legend, repeated by several writers, tells of a vast forest of oak and chestnut on Borough Moor, two miles south of Westminster. In the twelfth century the tithes of chestnuts in the Forest of Dean were granted to the monastery of Flaxley.

Chestnut palings are still popular for rough fencing. The wood resists the weather for decades. Chestnut is the only form of coppice that is really profitable. H. L. Edlin, writing in 1956, stated that there are '50,000 acres of chestnut coppice, most of it in the far south eastern counties of Kent, Surrey, Sussex and Hampshire... Roughly half this area carries standard trees' – usually of oak. This he takes as evidence of long-sustained artificial control. The shoots can grow six feet in a season. The wood from the coppices seems to have been put to most of the uses of ash, hop poles being probably a major demand, before the use of wire. The timber is an alternative to oak, perhaps a cheaper one, for the wood is shaky, i.e., it splits. Many old buildings were once thought to have chestnut beams, which on expert examination turned out to be of oak. Wine barrels are supposed to be best made of chestnut, and I have seen a barn in Sussex thatched with chestnut.

The tree is easy to recognise: the trunk, when old, is patterned with light brown ridges and furrows, which usually twist, right or left (but sometimes do not twist at all, especially in forest trees). The leaves are among the largest, simply boat-shaped, and with distinctive sharp serrations. The twig in winter is thick, with the buds forming out of sculptured channels. But there are exceptions to these descriptions: the twigs can be quite thin and the bark of young trees is a plain grey. In fact the trees in Britain are variable. The sweet or Spanish chestnut is *Castanea sativa*.

There is little difference between the Far Eastern, American and 'Spanish' species. The Japanese is a smaller tree. The Chinese, *C. mollisima,* can resist a fearsome bark fungus which destroyed nearly all American chestnuts in the first half of this century. The disease can attack the European species.

A chestnut which still stands and proliferates was once said to be the biggest tree in Britain: the Tortworth Chestnut. In 1766, it measured 50 feet in circumference. It is supposed, by some, to be about a thousand years old. In fact it is more like a giant beetroot than a tree, several stems coming from the bole, quite near the ground. Tortworth is between Gloucester and Bristol.

An even bigger tree, on Mount Etna, was hollow and big enough to contain a flock of sheep. Later it was discovered to be really five trees sharing the same root. A house was built inside, where chestnuts were dried in a kiln, fired by wood chopped from the inside of the tree(s).

Chestnut wood was put to a strange use during the last war, when large palings were carried to foreign shores by landing craft and unrolled on the beaches. The ancient Britons made the same sort of thing to cross marshes, but not with chestnut.

*chestnut plantatation, early spring, Ashridge, Herts*

*field elms near Sheering,
Essex : September sunrise*

# THE ELMS

The great trees which are so much a part of the brooding, fertile, hedge-patterned midland plains, are in fact a mysterious collection of species and hybrids, subject to diseases and inclined to drop large branches unexpectedly. These are the field elms, whose boles spring into tiny leaf, whose seeds are rarely fertile, yet they earned the title of Worcester Weed.

The English elms are:

|  | Smooth-leaved Elm | *Ulmus nitens* or *carpinifolia* (Common Elm) Europe |
|---|---|---|
| with leaves rough above: | Wych Elm | *U. glabra* (Scots Elm). Northern Europe |
|  | Dutch Elm | *U. major* or *hollandica*. A cross between the first two |
|  | Lock Elm | *U. minor* or *diversifolia* (Plot's Elm) East Anglia and Hampshire |
|  | English Elm | *U. procera* (Common Elm) |
| with smooth leaves, but tall, narrow shaped trees | Cornish Elm | *U. stricta*. S.W. England and Brittany |
|  | Jersey Elm | a variety with erect branches like a Lombardy poplar |

All but the first three are local in distribution, but the specific *procera* (tall) is often used to include all the 'field elms'. There are other elms in America and Asia. Some people believe that the wych elm is the only native British elm. It was almost certainly this elm which spread with, and sometimes before, the oak, after the birch and pine had colonised postglacial northern Europe.

In the pollen records the elms cannot be distinguished one from another, but the ancient elm is assumed to have been *U. glabra*, because of this species' present wide distribution in northern Europe, its fertility and hardiness. It is also the only elm native to Ireland. The elm continues in strength alongside the oak in the pollen diagrams, until about 3,000 B.C. when it begins to disappear. It revived and continued as a member of the forest community, but not in any strength. I suppose it is possible that some unidentified species died out to be replaced to some extent by the wych elm.

The succinct name, 'elm decline', is given to the prehistoric phenomenon, which was accompanied possibly by local climate change but, more remarkably, by the work of man. Temporary clearings are proved by the presence of plantains and other weeds of cultivation – for the first time in any quantity. Clearings reverted to forest, for the early cultivators were nomadic and moved on when the soil was exhausted. Oaks, sometimes removed with the elms, increased, and hazel continued with fluctuations which are its characteristic in the pollen diagrams. Lime, an important tree in the prehistoric forest, suffered similar variations. But the evidence points to neolithic clearing of elmwoods, perhaps on higher ground, or to a method of exploiting mixed woodland which was particularly injurious to the elm. Experiments were made in 1953, using stone axes from the Copenhagen Museum, to prove that early men could have cleared the forest. Everyone knows that thousands of these axes have been found.

Elms of all kinds have been used for winter fodder for cattle until recent times, and one reason, besides sporadic clearance, given for the decline of the elm, is that neolithic man kept cattle in forest conditions and cropped the trees to feed them. Another explanation which has been put forward is a possible epidemic of Dutch elm disease! The elm decline occurred in a mild, wet climate, and some sort of fungal attack, accelerated by vigorous lopping, cannot be ruled out.

*12. Lopped-Elm*

*eighteenth century engraving after Alexander Cozens shows that 'shredding' or lopping the foliage was still common*

*right : flowers of elm in February*

*opposite : English elms*

*fruit and young leaves of wych elm*

The wych elm still does make small woods along northern river valleys, and there is a wood in Cornwall. This species can be found growing wild on limestone in oak and ashwoods, and even on the chalk. Many woods that survived into historic times, of wych elm, ash or the native small-leaved lime, must have been killed by demands for fodder – when herds increased beyond the resources of local grazing, or a dry summer left the grass poor.

Weeping wych elms are common in old gardens and parks. The wych elm has large leaves, up to seven inches long, on thickish twigs whose shoots, almost at right angles to the twig, are hairy. The tree has a wide, spreading form and does not produce suckers from the bole and roots as do the other elms. This and the smooth bark of younger trees, is what must have earned it the name *glabra;* not the leaves. The bark of old trees is somewhat stringy. The only other elm tree which has a wide distribution in Europe is the smooth-leaved (or hornbeam-leaved) *U. carpinifolia.* The leaves are rather narrow and quite large, about four inches long. Its other scientific name, *nitens,* refers to the shiny quality of the leaves.

Elms have alternate leaves unequal at the base. All have pink or red

*the largest elm leaves are those of the wych elm, which is sometimes called the Scots elm*

flowers very early in the year, February or March, which turn into flat, round, winged nuts, ripening to various shades of brown in May as the leaves open. The bark of old trees is rugged, broken into irregular rectangles.

The wood of elms has always been extremely useful. Its important qualities are resistance to rotting, if kept wet (or dry), and its refusal to split. The first led to its use for drains, water pipes, pumps and buckets, and especially for coffins. The second made it ideal for the seats of chairs, which traditionally have beech legs and sticks, thrust into holes in the seat with a bent ash back, or hoop. The wood is brown, and its intricate grain is among the most attractive. Elm logs are poor firewood unless carefully dried.

The field elms were preserved in the hawthorn hedges of the enclosures; often planted there as a future source of timber. Odd elms can be found amongst oaks in spinneys and mixed woods of the midland and eastern counties. The hedgerows suit the elms, which grow to a great height on rich soil and clay, and flourish best in the open. They sometimes seed under the thorns. When they are cut down, the root suckers grow into new trees, which explains why you often see two or three very close together.

**Dutch elm disease**

Elm avenues were a fashion in eighteenth-century France, imitated here. Magnificently tall ones lined the Broad Walk in Kensington Gardens until about 1947, when they were all cut down, leaving a curious emptiness. Replanting of elms is discouraged by the ravages of Dutch elm disease, which periodically decimates the trees. It is caused by the elm-bark beetles, *Scolytus destructus* and *S. multistriatus*, formerly known together as *Scolytus scolytus*, which bring their own fungus food. This blocks the galleries eaten by the grubs and spreads into the cells of the tree, both choking and poisoning. The young beetles spread it to other trees. The signs of the disease are premature yellowing of the leaves and curling shoots.

A great elm at Crawley, on the London to Brighton road, was famous in early Victorian times. It was hollow to the top, with a circumference of 35 feet inside. There was a door into the tree and the floor was paved with bricks. Here a poor woman gave birth to a child, 'and afterwards remained there for a long time'. The lord of the manor held the key to the door. Another hollow elm, at Hampstead, had a spiral staircase in it and seats at the top for sightseers. In classical times, grape vines, thought to be parasites, were always trained on living elms, carefully pruned.

*outlines of common elms based on H. L. Edlin,* Know your Broadleaves

| Wheatley | smooth-leaved | Dutch | wych | English | Cornish |

*lonely hawthorn on
Haslingden Moor,
Lancashire*

# HAWTHORN

Two species of hawthorn, *Crataegus monogyna* and *C. oxyacantha*, are
native in Britain. The first is the common hawthorn or whitethorn of the
quickset hedge, and the second, sometimes called the midland hawthorn, is
less thorny and more shade-tolerant – a hawthorn of the woods. The two are
hybridised in the South and East, where they grow together. The name
*monogyna* means that the flower is one-styled (and the berry has only one
seed). *Oxyacantha* is simply a name for a thorn: the flowers of that species
have two or three styles. Cultivated garden hawthorns, with red flowers,
usually belong to this species. There are others, many others, for instance
an oriental hawthorn with yellow or orange berries. An old tree which
puzzled me for a long time, right on top of Parliament Hill, turned out to be
*Crataegomespilus*, a hybrid of hawthorn and medlar.

The history of the hawthorn in Britain goes back beyond the last Ice Age:
a single seed-stone from an interglacial deposit was given the elegant
name, *Crataegus clactonensis*.

Like several other shrubs and small trees, hawthorn began to spread
widely with the first forest clearances of neolithic man. It is a pioneer, which
on neglected land can form continuous scrub – often with a field layer of old
tins, to our shame. On the rich soil of old forest land the trees grow up into
small, gloomy woods, in which nothing else can grow. It is often seen as an
isolated bush or tree, protected by its thorns from the sheep – and very often
in the past protected by superstition. It may form scattered scrub on
southern hillsides or it may be an isolated tree in the middle of an Irish field,
or on top of a moor, as in the picture at the head. Hawthorn scrub is
sometimes coppiced. The timber is hard and fine-grained.

Hawthorns and their history are impregnated with magic and superstition
so varied as to result in opposing customs. For instance it is unlucky to bring

*May blossom*

**Pagan festivals**

hawthorn into the house: it may cause your mother's death. But in another county it may be hung over the chimney-piece on May Day to keep away evil spirits. In Ireland (and elsewhere) it was thought dangerous to cut a thorn tree, and this explains the presence of mature trees in unexpected places. Sometimes the trees were hung with rags and clothes for the fairies.

The May Queen, the prettiest girl in the village, was crowned with May blossom. By the old calendar, which held until 1751, May Day fell up to ten days later in the year, and the blossom was sure to be out by then. The May King, a dark figure, often completely shrouded in leaves, sometimes in a cage, was the Jack-in-the-Green often carved in old churches, but seldom mentioned. In many old rituals he was submitted to forms of sacrifice. Thus was the old year with its evils exchanged for the fertile new year, the young of the parish spending the previous night in the woods, and the day in dancing round the maypole. The maypole itself was a relic of tree-wakening rituals as well as a fairly clear phallic symbol.

Joseph of Arimathea, when he came to preach the gospel in Britain, landed on the (then) Island of Avalon. He stuck his thorn staff into the ground and slept. When he woke, his staff had blossomed; so he built a chapel there, which later became Glastonbury Abbey. Here the thorn and its descendants continued, and bloomed at Christmas. (When the calendar was changed it bloomed on Twelfth Night.) Many cuttings were taken from it, resulting in the variety, *praecox*, the Glastonbury thorn, which blooms in winter as well as in May.

Puritans attempted to cut down the tree, but it put their eyes out with its thorns, or the cutters went lame.

*the hawthorn's prickles protect it aginst grazing animals but are no hindrance to the blackbird*

*right : severely wind-cut hawthorn growing in a hole in the Burren limestone, County Clare*

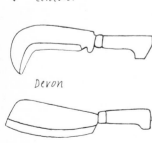

Cambridge

Leicester

Devon

Rutland

*billhooks*

But by John Evelyn's time there was a good trade in hawthorn seedlings for hedges, and the hedges were very much increased in the following centuries, as the land was enclosed from the commons by the landlords, and given over to sheep and economic farming. The custom of planting a standard tree: oak, elm, or ash, or in Herefordshire a crab apple, every twenty yards, was described by Evelyn and this pattern can still be seen. The hawthorn hedge was 'laid' every seven to ten years, the stems being half cut through and bent down: stakes of ash or oak were driven into the ground and loose branches interwoven. The top of the hedge was pleached with hazel rods or tied with strips of bark. One tool was used, the billhook, which varies in pattern from one county to another to suit the styles of the hedgers and the nature of the hedge. The art is not quite forgotten.

'Hedges' in Devon were made of large stones in two lines, the space between filled with earth, and standard trees were planted in the earth on top.

Roses and elderberries, brambles, and in the chalk many other shrubs, find their way into hawthorn hedges. It is said that you can tell the age of a hedge by the number of different species that compose it, additional to the original hawthorn. Typical herbs are cow parsley and others of that family, more or less poisonous; lords and ladies, in the shade; and Jack-by-the-hedge, or garlic mustard, the leaves delicious in sandwiches.

The haws are taken only by the birds who scatter the seeds and perpetuate the hawthorn – unless it is all grubbed up to make larger fields for the combines.

# HORNBEAM

This 'horny tree' grows wild only in the counties next to London, is scattered in the south and east generally and scarce or unknown in the north, in Scotland, Wales and Ireland: the most local of all the native trees. It is common in Europe and Western Asia and there are American and Japanese species. The nearest relations of *Carpinus betula* are the hazel and the birch, and not the beech, which it sometimes resembles at first glance.

The male catkins hang, with rows of umbrella-like bracts, and the female are erect at the end of the twig, with leaf-like bracts. The fruit has an unmistakable three-lobed wing. The leaves, which usually wait until early May, are folded along parallel veins, as are beech, but they are jagged-toothed instead of fringed with hairs, and placed more opposite than alternate on the twig. The trunk is smooth, grey, and always fluted or vertically streaked. Hornbeam casts a heavy shade, like the beech.

The tree was native to Northern Europe before the last Ice Age, and appears to have been abundant at some stages. It returned, perhaps only as an element of oakwoods in later postglacial times, always restricted to the S.E. William Morris, writing to the papers as an angry old man, in 1895, remembered from his youth, 'the biggest hornbeam wood in these islands' to have been in Epping Forest, which he knew 'yard by yard'. He inveighed against the 'experts of Epping' who he thought would ruin the forest by landscape gardening, tidying up the pollard hornbeams and straggling holly bushes.

The hornbeams of Epping (and Loughton) are still there, trees as emaciated as the present shape of the forest on the map. They, and beeches

*old pollard hornbeams*

*striated bark of a park hornbeam, Hampstead. Right: the winged fruit*

amongst them, are a wierd monument to an old necessity; the lopping of firewood from the living tree: a right which had to be fought for by the inhabitants of Loughton. The commoners had to establish their rights by beginning the job on 11 November, starting just after midnight. The landlord tried to get them drunk and forgetful on the tenth. Eventually he closed off the land. A firewood merchant trespassed, in 1866, with his sons, and they were imprisoned. One of the sons died in prison, of pneumonia. The people of Loughton went to law, while the landlord intrigued and tried to bribe the trespasser to leave the area. The case became a *cause célèbre*, seventeen landlords against the people of Loughton – who eventually won. Compensation of £7,000 they spent mostly on building a meeting place called the Loppers' Hall. The full account is given by J. H. Wilkes. Epping Forest now belongs to the City of London.

*hornbeam coppice*

There is quite a large acreage of coppice hornbeam in Kent, if it has not been converted to conifers. Some large trees, well-formed, are to be found in parks: a beauty grows in some wet gravel near the Hill Gardens on Hampstead Heath, and there are some large trees, over grass, in Hatfield Forest.

Hornbeams were once very fashionable for hedges and 'perplexed canopies' in gardens, as Evelyn tells with some enthusiasm for such 'blessed Elysiums'. In a more practical vein he describes the old value of hornbeam. Amongst other uses, it serves for mill-cogs, 'for which it excels either yew or crab; it makes good Yoke-timber... heads of beetles, stocks and handles of tools are made of it. It is likewise for the turner's use excellent. It makes good firewood, where it burns like a candle; and was of old so employed...' So it may have been called horn because it is hard, or because it made 'lant-horns'.

*the hornbeams of Loughton*

# IVY

The bonny ivy tree, which flourishes so vigorously in all our woods, is common from here to Asia Minor and is a member of the family Araliaceae, most of whose members are tropical. It flowers, oddly, in October and November, pollinated by and providing nectar for late-flying insects, including the larger butterflies. It is not really a tree of course: it is classed as a woody climber, with honeysuckle and traveller's joy. But unlike these two, its stem is often four or six inches thick, and even over twelve inches, and it has interesting habits of growth.

*lobed leaves of ivy
in winter*

Hedera helix is common in all deciduous woods, except the open birchwoods. It avoids very wet and very dry places and is limited by summer temperatures below 14°C, and winter temperatures below —1°C. It is not found in very acid, or very dry soil. It is a climber, not a parasite, and the only damage it does to trees is to limit their growth by smothering the bark and competing with the roots. Ivy climbs by means of adhesive short root-tendrils and needs a relatively flat surface – it does not strangle. It progresses along the floor until it finds a tree trunk or wall. Then it adapts to a vertical mode, using the small root-like fibres on the stem to cling. Once it reaches the light it can adopt a third method of growth, sending out shoots like a bush.

The leaves are typically three- or five-lobed until the final flowering shoots when they change to a simple pointed shape. The ivy is evergreen, but the leaves do go yellow sometimes. The berries form soon after the flowers and

*round heads of ivy flowers in late October*

*berries in January. Fruiting branches have unlobed leaves*

*climbing stems attach themselves to stone or tree bark by means of adhesive rootlets*

are often eaten by the birds before they turn black. They are supposed to be poisonous – but not to birds.

Ivy can cover the whole floor and all the trees in a wood, giving way only to ferns at the edges of a stream. In these circumstances the growth of new tree seedlings is probably discouraged. Trees heavy with ivy do seem to be somewhat sickly and I suppose their life is very much shortened. But assuming the growth of a wood to have been completely stifled by ivy, it is difficult to forecast the next stage. I cannot remember ever having seen a wood so ruined. Oaks in the wild, particularly, support the clinging stems as easily as they support many other plants: they grow old together. But ivy will always be discouraged by the forester, who needs the straightest timber.

On buildings, ivy is on balance good for the fabric, unless the brick or stonework is porous enough to accumulate soil. Then roots will form, which will expand and cause damage. But in the main, ivy will keep the wall dry, protect it from the sun and insulate it from frost. It will also add a romantic, soft outline; an air of the picturesque, which some people scoff at and others love – and must have done, when the Victorians manufactured tin ivy for instant conservatory cover.

Ivy leaves were a valuable food for cattle, though perhaps a last resort when all the elm leaves were used. Apart from this I can learn of no use that it was put to, and as for the Holly Boy and the Ivy Girl, I know nothing more than I told in the chapter on holly. Bacchus wore a crown of ivy, the Greeks had it at weddings, and Milton, to fill up a line, called it 'never sere'. A large-leaved variety is called Irish ivy and a small-leaved variety *japonica*. There are several cultivated, variegated sorts.

The American poison ivy is a sumach, no relation.

*elms and poplars along a Thames backwater. Water has affected the roots of the trees, but not those of the ivy which covers them*

# JUNIPER

*above : juniper berries take two or three years to form and ripen*

*right : juniper on the downs*

Usually a very small tree but with a surprisingly wide distribution and a long history. A dwarf form colonised the tundra in Britain immediately following the ice and still persists above the tree line in the Scottish Highlands. Juniper is an important and picturesque element of natural pinewoods (see the picture on p. 141). A lowland juniper wood is preserved in Dumfriesshire On the Chiltern escarpment there is quite a lot of juniper scrub, which is a natural precursor of beechwood. The photograph above was taken in Wiltshire; not all the trees have this fastigiate form. Holly bushes are the only other trees on this windswept hill.

The same tree, *Juniperus communis*, in various shapes, is found all over the northern hemisphere and well into the Arctic Circle. In America it grows to 30 feet. Our small trees are the remains of juniper scrub first established twelve thousand years ago. The ease with which the beech trees take root in its shade and then kill it with theirs, suggests that juniper scrub must once have occupied much of the high ground now under beechwoods. But palynologists have only recently learnt to distinguish its remains.

The wood was used for the handles of daggers and for spoons with a flavour of their own. The berries gave gin the only flavour it has, now produced by other means. Juniper is of the Pinacea family.

## LIME OR LINDEN

*above : looking up into the flowers of common lime*

The small-leaved lime, *Tilia cordata*, is our only undisputed native lime tree. It is rare. *Cordata* means heart-shaped. The large-leaved lime, *T. platyphyllos* is really based in warmer parts of Europe, but it is found wild in England The difference between the two trees is not so marked in the leaves as the names suggest, but the small-leaved species has more regular and round, less hairy and usually smaller leaves, from two to four inches long. Its flowers and the simple pear-shaped fruits which form in groups of about six, are almost erect, not hanging. The fruits of the large-leaved lime are less in number, and pendulous, but not heavily so. The individual fruits are ribbed. All lime trees can be large and have grey bark with vertical marks – line tree was once the English version of the name, which is *Linden*, in German, basswood in America.

What is known as the common lime, *T. vulgaris*, is a hybrid of the large- and small-leaved parents. It was imported enthusiastically, like tulips, from Holland, in the seventeenth century, and, like elms, planted in avenues – which can be seen all over the country. Very large lime trees were famous before this – one in Germany was so large that it had to be supported by a hundred props.

No particular use is made of the timber, but most of Grinling Gibbons'

*lime seedling*

carving was done in lime wood – it can't be bad. The timber of the American lime, called basswood, is important. An Indian member of the Tiliaceae family produces jute. Lime-flower tea is said to be drinkable, and bees collect the copious nectar. The leaves are peculiarly subject to aphid attack, but before the insects get there, are usable in salads. The limes used in making lime-juice are in fact citrus fruits and no relation.

The early history of the smalled-leaved lime is curious. It seems to have been an important tree, at least one in twenty other trees, in the Atlantic period around 4,000 B.C. when the climate was still warmer than it is now. It may have formed continuous woodland in favoured situations, as well as being scattered over the forest area, but not in Ireland. It declined, but not so rapidly as elm. Its decrease is consistent with a gradually cooling climate, and borne out by its present location in the protection of the Avon Gorge.

All the same, there is room for speculation. The decline of the lime did occur at the same time as a great increase in population in southern Britain. Neolithic farmers and builders could have found good uses for a tree which has edible leaves in spring and whose bark can be made into ropes, nets or mats – and even clothing. To get a long fibre whole trunks and branches must be stripped – very destructive to the trees. The bark easily forms ribbons of fibre which can be separated into strands. Bast weaving is still important in parts of China and Russia.

An agricultural people who herded animals, made pottery, traded axes, built and thatched wooden houses, would certainly know how to make use of every tree. Limes, quite possibly whole woods of lime, would not survive a constant demand for bark. The cooling climate, and the presence of grazing animals, did not encourage regeneration.

The relatively small numbers of lime trees that survived into the medieval forests were equally vulnerable and the species became a rarity. Even the introduced hybrid, though it produces numerous seedlings, does not gain any ground. Edlin points out that Lyndhurst, in the New Forest, probably means Linden-clearing, and, he says, a lime seedling would get short shrift from the ponies there.

*the double avenue at Clumber Park, Notts*

*field maple in autumn*

## MAPLES

Maples are famous the world over for brilliant autumn colours. The humble native field maple, so often cut back into the hedge, is not perhaps very remarkable, though it does sustain rich golds and reds in its leaves for several weeks up to December.

The leaves of this small tree, *Acer campestris*, are half the size of those of the much more common sycamore, and quite different in shape and texture – as are the twigs except for their symmetry. The winged fruits, however, are similar. Equally recognisable are the double fruits of another maple commonly planted in Britain but not really naturalised: the Norway maple, *A. platanoides*. Thus we have three maples with five-lobed leaves, yellow-green flowers and winged fruit. They are easy enough to distinguish, but a summary may be useful:

| *Acer campestris* | *A. platanoides* | *A. pseudoplatanus* |
|---|---|---|
| native | planted | alien, but rampant |
| **field or common maple** | ***Norway maple*** | ***sycamore*** |
| flower clusters erect | flowers erect | flowers hanging |
| with the leaves | before the leaves | under the leaves |

wings horizontal    wings curved back    wings curved in

The sycamore is described on page 104. Japanese maples, planted for their colours in gardens, may have many-lobed or very sharply pointed or compound or very deeply lobed leaves. An American tree called, curiously, box elder, is an *Acer* with three-foliate, unevenly toothed leaves and pretty hanging clusters of flowers on the bare twigs in April.

Field maple trees grow up to 35 feet high, but can be twice that. The bark is dull brown, sometimes raised in corky fluting to give a star-shaped section to the smaller branches. The wood turns well and it was once used in making rare bowls – and for inlays. The grain is close with a delicate pattern. Birds-eye maple, a type of figured veneer, comes from this tree and from the American sugar maple – also the source of maple syrup. Maple-wood tables were valuable collectors' items in the Roman world: one was sold for its weight in gold.

Records of the field maple go back to the Neolithic period – no further. It was another fodder tree. Mapuldur was the form of the Old English name, and christened two 'hams' – in Oxfordshire and Hampshire. The distribution of the tree has always been towards the south and east, on limestone and chalk.

The Norway maple is native to all Europe except western France and Britain. It can be a bigger tree than the field maple and is more regular in form than the sycamore. Its bark is darker than either. It is planted for ornament – the leaves turn golden yellow. The beautiful greenish-yellow flowers emerge from bulging buds which fold back pink satiny scales: the leaves, pink-stained at first, follow soon after.

*field maple twig with corky bark*

*park maple in autumn*

*Norway maple*

*aspen trunk with root suckers*

# POPLARS

The black poplar and the aspen are definitely native to Britain; the grey poplar is said to be. More visible are three alien trees, commonly planted: the Lombardy poplar, which is a variety (*italica*) of the black; the strangely named black Italian, which is a cross between the European and Canadian black poplars; the white poplar or abele, similar to the grey, but with leaves, some of them lobed, that remain white until they decay.

In addition to these six species is a large range of hybrids, usually planted in neat rows with the aid of government grants. They are usually, I believe, based on the black poplar. Strains are developed which can be grown beautifully straight and quickly, and are well adapted to poor, wet soils. They provide shelter belts, screens for buildings and industrial eyesores, and produce straight timber at the same time.

*short back and sides for a town poplar*

All poplars hybridise easily and new ones are being developed, so recognition is far from easy: even the experts seem to give conflicting accounts. All poplars have lovely, dark red catkins and green female ones like strings of beads – less so with aspen, which has generally hairy catkins. Female trees of the cultivated forms are unpopular because of their downy seeds.

Poplar genera are divided, by Makins, into groups by their leaves:
1. leaves without translucent border, stalk flattened (*Populus tremula*, the aspen) 2. leaves with translucent border, stalk flattened (*P. nigra*, black poplar; *P. monilifera* or *canadensis,* Canadian black poplar, or cottonwood) 3. leaves white or grey, felted below (*P. canescens*, grey and *P. alba*, white) 4. leaves without translucent border and stalk not flattened or only slightly

99

*aspen leaves*

so. These last are the balsam poplars of N. America and China, sometimes called the tacamahaca group, and include *P. candicans,* the Balm-of-Gilead, also called cottonwood. Not only the species are complicated; the names are too.

The common aspen is a moderate-sized tree with round wavy-edged or toothed leaves which are in constant motion. It has purple hairy catkins in February and downy fruiting catkins in May. Aspens are widely distributed over the whole of Britain and Ireland, but supposed to be more common in the S.E. By suckering they form small groups of trees, whispering together.

The native black poplar is mostly restricted to stream-sides and wet woodland in the east and south Midlands. There is nothing especially black about it, but the bole is rugged and often has swellings with short shoots growing from them. The stem is vertical and the branches irregular, starting low on the trunk. The leaves are of the rounded triangle and diamond shapes familiar from the Lombardy poplar.

*left : male catkins of black Italian poplar. Right : female catkins of white poplar. Below : black poplar leaf*

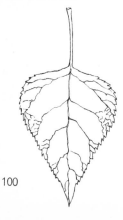

Lombardy poplars, (*P. nigra* var. *italica*) are planted everywhere and need no description. This is a fastigiate form which, unusually, grows easily from cuttings.

Black 'Italian' poplars (*P. serotina* means late leafing) have triangular leaves and a very recognisable fan-shaped outline. They are often very big, and never female. One popular variety of this popular hybrid has beautiful golden yellow leaves.

The grey poplar has a distribution mostly in woodland, similar to that of the black poplar. It has some characteristics of the aspen and is sometimes said to be an ancient hybrid of these two trees. The leaves are wavy-edged and vary from round to roughly pointed, but not lobed. The grey down on the underside is reduced in the summer. The bark above the black bole is a clear light grey with black streaks.

*hybrid poplars grown as a crop*

*below : Lombardy poplars planted as a windbreak*

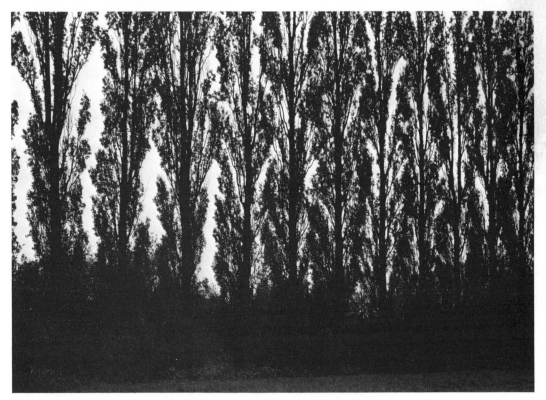

*new leaves of black
Italian poplar*

The white poplar is commonly seen as a planted tree in towns and country in the south. Its bark is usually yellow-grey and patterned with symmetrical lenticels, above the dark, broken part on the bole. The leaves are always downy below, right until they fall, and very variable in shape, with large lobed ones at the ends of shoots and at the top of the tree. The vernacular name of the white poplar used to be 'abele', perhaps a corruption of *alba*.

The timber of poplar is soft, white, does not splinter and is slow to burn. It is used, so they say, for matchsticks and wagon bottoms. In paper-thin sheets (veneers) cut from the circumfrence as for plywood, it makes punnets and camembert boxes. Dutch clogs are made of poplar. From packing cases to the backs of drawers, from floors to toys, there are plenty of uses for this soft, straight-grained timber.

*regular diamond-shaped
markings are typical of
white poplars, and also
found on parts of the bark
of grey poplars. Right :
autumn leaves of white
poplar showing variations
in shape and persistent
whitish colour*

# ROWAN

The rowan, or mountain ash, much loved by early Celtic poets for its scented, creamy blossom, and by birds for its berries, is a *Sorbus*: thus of the same genus as the whitebeams and the wild service tree and a member of the great rose family. It is a little tree usually, elegant in shape – so tenacious as to grow from almost vertical bank sides, and popular in gardens because it keeps to itself. I have seen a very big rowan in Ross-shire. It had probably been preserved as a landmark – it was at a remote crossroads – but it was surrounded by electric wires.

This is a native of north and west Britain, a mountain tree as its name says, and I think an escape from gardens in the south. Called witchen or wiggin, it was a certain protection against witches and was often planted round homesteads, and in Wales even in churchyards. A cross or loop of the twigs was enough to protect you or your animals, while the use of the timber for butter churns was a reasonable precaution. It is a fine, close-grained wood, but not available in large sections.

rowan and hazel on a steep
valley side in western
Scotland

*arbutus amongst holly
and oak, County Kerry*

# THE STRAWBERRY TREE

In the incomparable surroundings of the lakes of Killarney grows this beautiful evergreen tree with fleshy round fruits on stalks, and bell-shaped flowers which appear in autumn. It is found also in W. Cork and nowhere else in Britain, unless planted in gardens, where it remains small. It is *Arbutus unedo*, a native of Portugal and South Europe.

It is earnestly claimed as one of several native plants surviving in the Lusitanian climate of this warm, moist, protected corner; but it is strange that no arbutus pollen has survived in the peat which fills the valley floors and covers much of the mountainsides. The arbutus trees are rooted amongst the rocks, with a minimum of protection and a maximum of light. The trunk is sinuous and brown, and the bark resembles the matted fur of an animal, though it peels off in places. Most of the trees on the ridges are dying and many twisted trunks lie about as if the rocks had cracked in a severe frost – which is unlikely here. But regeneration does not seem to occur, and the rich green of the leaves is often spoilt by black rust spots. There are healthier trees in the small nature reserve of nearby Muckross, but I cannot say they have the same romantic appeal.

*young leaves of sycamore
are tinged with red, like
other maples*

# SYCAMORE

The sycamore is an alien maple, *Acer pseudoplatanus*, which now far
outnumbers the native field maple. Known to Gerard in the late sixteenth
century as the rare Great Maple, planted for its shade on noblemen's
estates, it soon became a fashionable tree. It was thought to have been the
fig-mulberry – called sycomorus in the Bible – which Zaccheus climbed to
watch Christ ride into Jerusalem, and people wanted to have it near their
houses. It was found to provide good timber and firewood and good shelter
from winds and sun. The sap, bled from the trunk, could be used in making
ale, with a great saving of malt, but I don't know how much this influenced
the choice.

Now it grows and reproduces everywhere in the British Isles, as far north
and as far west as you find any trees; and in the most exposed situations it
grows straight. It was planted to shelter farm buildings high on the moors.
Here it flourishes on the rich manure leaking from the farmyard, and is only
shaped, not bent, by the wind. It is a valuable forest tree and is grown in
plantations, for instance in Yorkshire, where its wood was used until
recently to make the clean, rigid rollers used in textile mills. The sycamore's
highest concentration is in west Yorkshire and south Lancashire. Here it
comes closest to forming woods, crowding on the sour banks of old mills,
flashes and roads, and pieces of wasteland, and filling the ragged cloughs
on the edges of moors with shade, while helping to prevent further erosion.
It creeps into the edges of woods unaggressively: using the protection of
other trees to start its growth, but then taking its place. It is a lesson in
successful immigration.

The seedlings of sycamores are everywhere in May, two green wings with
at first no hint of the five-lobed leaf: then a pair of pointed, serrated leaves.
The bark is grey and the trunk slightly muscular and nobbly: smooth at first
then maturing into ragged flakes, which rarely fall. The buds are green, full

105

*wind-shaped sycamores on the site of an old farm building on the Yorkshire moors*

and sharply symmetrical in scale markings and on the twigs. The flowers, opening from satiny pink buds, soon after the leaves, hang – unlike the other maples which grow here – and are in panicles of up to 100, females above and males below. Heavy nectar provides early food for the bees. Several pairs of fruits are forming while the lower flowers are still in bloom. The winged fruits are nearly at right angles to each other. They separate to become aerodynamically balanced, as gliding autogiros, almost certain to reach the ground some way from the tree. In fact they must often be carried 200 yards or more by high winds, for trees to migrate as they do. The slightly sticky leaves collect a lot of aphids when the tree grows in unexposed places.

*below : flowers budding in a gale. Right : two weeks later fruits are forming*

sycamores, above, in
western Ireland ; below : in
Lancashire

*below : bark
covered in green algae*

*fading leaves by a
Lancashire reservoir*

The spread of sycamores in Britain in 'modern' times is exactly parallel to that of several native trees which reached us from central and southern Europe supposedly unaided by man. If anything, it is more vigourous and adaptable, but it does not threaten any serious alteration of the ecology, either locally or nationally. Its only well-known fungus disease, the tar spot of sycamore leaves, is actually reduced by the sulphurous air of its more industrial habitats. It is in fact as familiar all over Britain as the field elms in lowland England, and less at risk.

**Wood for fiddles**

Sycamore wood is a pale creamy colour, and when polished shows a lustrous wavy pattern. Specially selected pieces are invariably used for the back, belly and sides of any stringed instrument of the violin family.

Trees used for timber are usually cut at 50 to 80 years old. Very large, old trees are known and have entered into local history – and even national, in the case of the Martyrs' Tree in Tolpuddle, Dorset; a sycamore preserved with help from the TUC. The agricultural labourers used to meet under the tree in the 1830's in, then, illicit union, and were savagely punished in 1834. Trees as old as 300 years will usually have been pollarded. Grown properly they can reach 125 feet, but need fertile soil with some lime content.

A shapeless old sycamore near Mountrath, Co Laois, is called St Finton's Well. The original holy well was filled in, but the water appeared in the centre of the tree. Hundreds of Irish pennies have been beaten into the bark by passers-by, as offerings.

There are several varied types of leaf in cultivated forms: yellow, and variegated with white or yellow, and one with a sort of blackcurrant pink on the undersides.

*finely patterned trunk of a walnut in Cambridge*

# WALNUT

The walnut family includes the hickory trees of America and the Caucasian wing-nut, which may sometimes be seen in parks. All have leaves rather like the ash, but set not quite opposite on the stalk. The walnut is itself a native of the Caucasus mountains. The scientific name, *Juglans*, is the old Roman name (Jupiter's nut) and perhaps has the same roots as jugal, (yoked) and conjugal (yoked together in marriage) for it always seems to have been connected with marriage. Roman bridegrooms threw walnuts to the children, and Evelyn describes an old German custom, near Frankfurt, whereby a young man had to prove his worth by the walnut trees he possessed or had planted. This at least ensured the continuance of this valuable tree in the district. 'Burgundy' says Evelyn, 'abounds in them, where they stand in the midst of goodly wheat-lands'.

**Crop forecaster**  In England, where they might have been brought by the Romans, but were certainly increased by returning crusaders, they are usually to be seen by old farmhouses. They supply walnuts for pickling and act as long range weather-forecasters for the crops. Being at the edge of their natural area of distribution, they are particularly sensitive to frost and wind in May. The crop of fruit is variable, for the male catkins are often out of step with the

*walnut twig*

*below : walnuts growing wild with dogwood scrub and traveller's joy in a dry valley of the Chilterns*

female flowers; this would ensure cross-pollination in a walnut wood, but is a hindrance to a lonely tree. The habit of beating walnut trees is to encourage the faster production of flowering shoots by breaking the branches.

In the rest of Europe, walnuts are grown for their timber, which, before mahogany was imported, was the finest known. (It still is, in spite of mahogany.) The wood is used for gun stocks as it was during the Napoleonic Wars. A good tree would fetch £600 – a small fortune. There were plantations in Surrey at one time : but Edlin describes it as 'exacting' in soil and situation. Even so, it will sometimes grow wild, and I know a grove of (not too healthy) walnuts in exactly the situation described by Evelyn as suiting them: chalky, rich land protected from heat or cold 'as in great pits', or valleys. Rooks are possibly the only birds capable of spreading the nuts.

Pickling them green or keeping them dried for Christmas were not the only ways of eating walnuts. The fresh nuts can be scooped out of their shells, with salt and vinegar, and for a sweet they can be boiled in sugar when still green. Walnut oil can be used in cooking. It is a 'drying oil' like linseed oil, and was often preferred by painters, because it dries slowly and goes less brown. 'Nut oil' can still be bought, but more painters value the speed of acrylics.

# WHITEBEAM AND WILD SERVICE

Adjacent alphabetically and botanically these two small trees do in fact hybridise as *Sorbus eminens*, found only in the Wye and Avon valleys. Numerous other variant whitebeams are dignified (or otherwise) as species with some curious names, and are local in Devonshire, Ireland, the Mendips, Brecon and the Isle of Arran respectively or plurally.

The common whitebeam, *S. aria*, is a modest tree of the chalk scrub, in spring looking as white as the junipers look black. It is also found in ashwoods. It seems to be the southern counterpart of its close relation, the rowan, and is a native of S. Europe and its mountains. Nothing much is

*flowers of Whitebeam*

*autumn leaves of Swedish whitebeam*

known about its postglacial history, no doubt partly because it grows in chalk. The variations in leaf, from oval and toothed, to jagged and maple-like in the wild sevice, are matched by the whiteness under the leaves. An intermediate form, sensibly called *S. intermedia*, is the Swedish whitebeam; a planted, often fairly large tree sometimes found wild – and gorgeous in autumn. A small whitebeam of Arran seems to be close to it. A Devonshire whitebeam, or service tree of the south-west and S.E. Ireland, produced berries for the market, called 'French hales'.

**The wild service tree**     The wild service tree is so called to distinguish it from the service-berry, a cultivated member of the pear fraternity. 'Service' is a corruption of Sorbus. *S. torminalis*, the wild service, with large round buds, six or more pointed lobes to the leaves, and brown pruny fruits, is a native of East Europe and Southern Britain. It is rarely as large as its maximum 70 feet, and is rare anyway. It grows on clay in the south. The berries, eagerly taken by birds, were called chequers and eaten by people as a cure for colic.

*leaves and fruit of the wild service tree*

*pollard willows in flooding Thames near Abingdon*

## WILLOWS

Willows are very much a part of English life, providing cricket bats, decorative backgrounds for undergraduates, trugs for lady gardeners and artificial limbs for empire builders. But they were even more important in the rural economy.

The spread of the commonest of several native species has been very much increased by planting along rivers, streams and ditches. The trees are, more often than not, pollarded. The supply of poles for fencing was

*Bedford willow in early leaf with catkins, April*

essential in low lying districts, where rich land was not wasted on hazel coppice. The old willow boles, rarely sound, and falling about untidily, continue to shoot vigorously and also to play their part in maintaining the banks of rivers; they are not destroyed by temporary flooding.

This common species is *Salix fragilis*, the crack willow. Large twigs will crack off just above the joint – an unusual method of natural propagation. You can in fact plant a willow by simply sticking a piece into the ground. The seeds are less reliable but will 'take' while fresh, in wet earth. This European tree has been planted in N. America, and is now completely naturalised there.

The white willow, *S. alba*, is the other large riverside tree, more common in East Anglia and the east Midlands. It was formerly called the Huntingdon willow. The backs of the leaves are distinctly white. A variety of the white willow is grown under controlled conditions for making cricket bats. The straight trees are felled at between twelve and twenty years old. The hybrid of the crack and white willows is the Bedford willow, used for wooden legs.

Some forms of white willow are weeping trees. The real weeping willow, *S. babylonica*, hardy, with bright yellow twigs, said to have been brought from the Euphrates in the eighteenth century, is in fact a native of China.

*cricket bat blank*

*opposite : white willow by the River Nene, Northants*

By the waters of Babylon, the Israelites sat down and wept under *Populus euphratica*, we are told. There are many forms of the weeping willow, which has the shortest winter of any tree, sometimes keeping its old leaves until January and putting out catkins and small leaves in April.

The bay willow, *S. pentandra*, has broader, dark leaves and bushy fruiting catkins. It is usually a bush but can grow large. This is a native willow of the northern parts of Great Britain and Ireland. Its southern counterpart is perhaps the almond willow, with narrow leaves and flaking brown bark: but it is usually shrubby.

All the several species besides these five are large or small shrubs. They can be classified roughly as osiers, goat willows and dwarfs.

Before easy transport led to the centralising of industries, each district had its osier bed, where the trees were cropped annually for withies to be made into baskets. The common osier, *S. viminalis*, with very long leaves, grey below, is the best tree, but other willows were also useful. The cropping and treatment of the sticks, and their weaving into many kinds of basketry, are highly skilled and technical. The industry is now centred on Sedgemoor, in the Somerset Levels.

Pussy willow, goat willow, or sallow, *S. caprea*, with common or grey sallow, *S. cinera*, are commonly quite small: much torn and hacked by people and goats. The goat willow or great sallow can grow into a moderate sized tree. Eared sallow, *S. aurita*, is also a pussy willow, in the north: it has miniature leaves or ears at the base of the leaf stalk. All three pussy willows have quite broad leaves with wrinkles above and down below. Sallows, unlike other willows, are found in woodland.

*characteristic downy, veined underside of sallow leaf*

*silvery leaves and hairy seeds of the creeping willow, S.Lancashire coast. Bunches of thick, fluffy seeds are also typical of sallows*

The smaller willows are something of a specialist study. Easy to recognise is the silvery creeping willow of old sand dunes and fens, *S. repens*. Usually about knee-high, it is supposed to grow into a bush in some places. The

*male flowers, left, and
female, right, of sallows
are on separate trees*

*below : sallows fill a
valley between larch
plantations. Devon*

similar downy willow grows in the mountains. English names of the others are descriptive: all grow in the Scottish Highlands. They are Woolly, Whortle-leaved, Plum-leaved, Net-leaved and Least. The last, *S. herbacea*, grows at the highest altitudes and never raises itself from the ground or snow.

It was this plant, of all the trees, with mountain avens, docks, goosegrass, cornflowers and several arctic plants, which crept over the raw soil behind the melting ice, 12,000 years ago. Leaves of least willow of this age have been found, rolled up in mud, in Cornwall, Essex, Galway and Dublin. It grows now in the arctic regions and on the Alps, and is not uncommon in the Scottish Highlands and on some Welsh and Irish mountain tops. The warm conditions of the later postglacial period, which encouraged other trees, wiped it out of the lowlands. The other small willows and sallows have almost as long a history, and originally colonised particular soils and regions not necessarily similar to their present habitats, where many are confined by their intolerance of summer heat. The larger willows have no ascertainable history before the Bronze Age.

All willows have easily recognised twigs, with alternate single-scaled buds, like claws, and all have catkins, which appear early, before the leaves or with the first leaves. The sallows and most of the others have male and female catkins on separate trees. All willows are at least partly pollinated by insects and the early catkins of sallow were especially valuable to bee-keepers when cheap sugar was not available. The bark of larger trees is distinctively ribbed and usually a light, greenish brown.

**Willow crafts**

The timber of the willow is white, like that of the poplars, which are of the same family, Salicaceae. It provides few great logs for the sawmills. Its virtues are lightness and flexibility and these have made it immensely useful ever since man first built shelters and coracles or made fishing nets and fences. It can be split and cleft into strips so fine that they can be woven into cloth, and even ropes. The bark was used for tanning and deep red dyes were made from the roots. The poles of three or four years growth were as much used for handles of pitchforks and rakes as the tougher ash in other districts. The rapid growth of willows was especially admired and valued. Hurdles, sieves, fruit baskets and beehives were made from thin, cleft willow wood and small timber was used for carriages, boxes of all sorts and clogs. The best wood, from the white willow, was used for milk pails. Well dried, the wood was considered to be good fuel, nearly smokeless. Willow charcoal, in thin sticks, is still produced for art students.

Sallows, especially for hop-poles, could be grown on poor ground, but osiers were planted by the acre, in fertile, damp, but carefully drained soil. Osier beds contained not only the long-leaved osier itself, but other species such as purple willow and numerous varieties and hybrids. They all had names, such as Yellow Osier, Snake or Speckled and Green Osier, Old Basket Osier, Welsh Wicker, Horse Gelster, Whining Gelster, Hard, Soft and Fine Golstones and Golden and Green Willow. No doubt there were many other local names, never written down.

The uses of basketry and wickerwork were obviously much greater when cheap metal alloys and wire, imported softwoods and jute, not to mention plastics, were not available. Even today we have lobster pots, hampers, skips and vegetable containers of all sorts, chairs, cradles, shopping baskets and hats all made of various degrees and qualities of willow, as well as of reeds, and of course, many substitutes. The mellow colour of good baskets is produced by boiling the wood before the bark is removed.

Baskets and trugs can also be made of oak, pine, poplar and alder. The shoots of hazel, poplar and rowan, too, can be used to weave baskets.

**Pain killer**

Willows were known since classical times to have a medicinal value and decoctions of the leaves were used to treat local pains. The juice is extremely bitter and seems not to have been included in the many and complex herbal medicines, though Culpeper recommended it, with wine, for spitting of blood, consumption and 'staying the heat of lust' in men or women. In the nineteenth century it was known to contain salicine, from which salicylic acid was made, used in skin complaints. A material called Peruvian Bark was used as a pain killer. At the end of the century a German chemist isolated acetyl-salicylic from willow bark. This is, in fact, aspirin.

Neat round galls in the branches of crack willows are the homes of the maggots of a gnat; more untidy ones, formed from the catkins, are made by a gall mite. A sawfly engineers bean galls on leaves, and others cause a whole range of cunning distortions of the leaf.

*garden willows going 'wild' on the banks of an electric railway in N. London*

# 4 – NATIVE SHRUBS

The difference between a tree and a shrub is not just one of size, though shrubs are usually no more than ten or fifteen feet high. The vegatative processes of trees and shrubs are the same, but shrubs do not develop a single leading shoot which would form the trunk of a tree: they grow several stems. If some are damaged or eaten, they can continue to grow. Their low stature enables them to exist in windswept places – where, in fact, some trees also adopt shrubby forms. Scrub largely consists of shrubs.

Many shrubs can adapt, or may have originated, as the 'shrub layer' of the forest: but they can grow better in full light and are able to colonise open grassland or soils taken over by herbaceous plants. Some die off completely when forest trees grow above them. All are treated as weeds by foresters. Some small trees, like hazel, hawthorn and holly, are usually seen in shrubby form simply because they have been usually coppiced, or are cut as hedges. Most species of willow are shrubs or less, but it would have been confusing to separate them from the tree species.

barberry

**Barberry** This was a common native shrub distinguished by triple, forked spines and oval red berries, edible; but it forms an essential host to part of the life-cycle of wheat rust fungus and has therefore been weeded out by farmers. Other *Berberis* species escape from gardens.

**Blackthorn** A prunus, well known for its white flowers in early April, sometimes well before the leaves, in a 'blackthorn winter'. The berries are sloes; really small bitter plums, with stones and typical whitish bloom on the blue-black skin. Sloe gin is merely gin flavoured with sloes. The hard wood with its polished bark is used for sticks and the short shillelaghs still sold to tourists in Ireland. Blackthorn is common in the hedge, where it characteristically sends out long shoots. It can form dense thickets and grows everywhere except the Highlands. *Prunus spinosa*.

**Alder buckthorn** A useful, little noticed, shrub of wet land, this buckthorn is not thorny, nor is it related to the alder; but it grows with alders in the type of wet woodland named alder carr. Its uses were for dyes from the berries (which ripen through green and red to black); purgative bark; and a modern use – very fine charcoal for slow fuses. The simple, slightly wavy leaves, with parallel veins, are alternate, but nearly opposite; the flowers small and green, rather scattered on the twig. *Frangula alnus*, or *Rhamnus frangula* according to Linnaeus.

*broom and gorse*

**Broom** Not spiny, but with complex narrow leaves and yellow flowers, it is often associated with gorse to which it is related as one of the Leguminosae. Its seeds are in hairy pods about 2 inches long. It grows on good acid soils and hedge banks. A weed to foresters it is none the less useful in encouraging the growth of conifers, possibly because, like other leguminous plants, it adds nitrogen to the soil. It is sometimes planted on the sides of motorway cuttings. There are garden varieties of *Cytisus scoparius*.

**Buckthorn** This is purging buckthorn, a near relation of the Californian cascara. The berries, quite black, are purgative, but people could not always wait for the berries and the inner bark was used – not too fresh, for it can cause pains and vomiting. 'The outer bark contrarywise,' says Culpeper, 'doth bind the body.' This shrub grows only in chalk hills. The thorns, 'bucks' horns', are blunt, and terminal in the branches, which fork symmetrically. The green flowers, similar in either sex, but on different trees, form in clusters, axillary in the radiating groups of leaves, which have pronounced curving veins and lightly serrated edges. *Rhamnus carthatica*.

**Dogwood** A *Cornus* with clearly recognisable red twigs. Leaves are very similar to buckthorn, but sharper pointed and smooth-edged. The flowers are white in close terminal clusters, the berries black – quickly removed by birds. Red pigment, always discernible in the plant, floods the leaves in autumn. Plentiful on the chalk and not unknown elsewhere: the sticks were used for butchers' skewers or 'dogs', said not to flavour the meat. But it may have been named because it *looked* like blood-stained skewers – certainly other wood was used. *Cornus sanguinea*.

*dogwood in the hedge in late autumn*

**Elder**  You can pickle the flower buds, or fry the flowers in batter – said to be delicious – infuse them as tea, or add them to fruit pies, as you can the berries, which also make excellent wine. The young buds, boiled in water, cured fevers and inflamations: with butter they were made into an ointment for aches and sprains. The inner bark was used to treat burns. An extract of the berries 'assisted longevity' and was a catholicon against all inflrmities. An infusion of the leaves was used as insecticide, and carters hung the leaves over their horses' heads to keep off the flies. In spite of all this the elder has always been unpopular. It had a bad name. It was a witches' tree. Judas was hanged from it. It must never be used to mend a child's cradle or the witches would have the child in their power. Some countrymen will not have it as a gift to

It was unlucky to have an elder near the house; besides, it has a nauseating smell – in Spain or somewhere the inhabitants of a house had been killed or diseased because it was surrounded by elders. Biting midges breed in the trees. Even the rabbits won't touch it, so it grew on rabbit warrens. There was an elder by the kitchen drain when I was a child, and I must say I disliked it. In fact it thrives on the rich manure of house and farm drains, and will often colonise rubbish dumps. The birds carry the seeds to odd corners everywhere and it can be seen in woods in attenuated, unflourishing form, the leaves slow to fall and early to break.

The twig is thick, pithy and warty. As a bush, elder is hard to remove: it is a good coppice tree.

Allowed to grow up, it forms a respectable tree, with very hard wood, apart from the pithy shoots.

13. *Elder*

*elder tree by Alexander Cozens. Right : tree in County Cork*

burn. If you must cut an elder, you must ask the 'Old Gal's' permission – she is the English version of the Scandinavian Elder Mother – a witch for sure; old Ellen.

It was used even for the cogs of mill machinery, especially where no hornbeam was available, and for all sorts of pegs and toys. Butchers who knew no dogwood preferred it for skewers. Evelyn: 'it is close grained, sweet and cleanly . . . least affecting their flesh.' Elder is *Sambucus*, the common elder *nigra*. There are several varieties, the oddest being *S. nigra* var *alba*.

Here is an old recipe for elderberry wine. To every gallon of the juice or berries, add two gallons of spring water. To every gallon of the liquor put 3 lb. of coarsest sugar. Let it stand for 10 or 14 days, stirring frequently (with an oaken rod) for the first four days. Take off the head. Add one gallon of best brandy to every 14 of the liquor and tun it. After it has fermented for several weeks and has done working, add some egg shells and paper down the cask; and in March you may rake it off from the lees, and put it back in the cask when it is cleaned, and let it stand 3 weeks, and if it is fine you may bottle it, though it would be much better to let it stand till October following. Bottled, cork it well and lay on its side to keep the cork wet.

This recipe can be used for other fruit as well. It is from Chambers' Pocket Herbal, 1800.

**Gorse** Linnaeus, according to the *Reader's Digest,* is supposed to have fallen to his knees to thank God for the sight of gorse on Putney Heath, and I felt something of his emotion when I first saw County Kerry: gorse in flower has that appeal. It is only called furze in Ireland, where it once had many uses, probably for lack of any other tree. Here, and in Scotland and Brittany, it was cut very early in the year and bruised as feed for cattle, horses and donkeys. It is supposed to be very good for them. It was also used for litter. The stems are good fuel to help the sluggish turf. Furze provided many useful bits of wood and as a bush was excellent for cleaning chimneys. In S.W. Ireland it has obviously been planted as hedges, though it grows wild everywhere, and it was used in earlier times to improve barren land – it is leguminous.

Gorse, furze or whin grows on heaths of all sorts, and on downs and cliffs, and blooms from January to June and after. This is *Ulex europaeus*. About June the flowers of *U. gallii* appear. This gorse or furze is a duller, paler green: in the west.

**Guelder rose** So called because its cultivated variety, the snowball tree, came from Dutch Guelderland, this is a common but widely scattered shrub with leaves like a maple and white flowers in flat clusters. The large flowers at the edges are without sexual equipment, being for advertisement only. The berries are bright red and the leaves go crimson. This is another skewer bush. *Viburnum opulus* grows on damp soil at the edges of woods and thickets.

*gorse hedges in Kerry*

**Privet** Wild privet is a spindly bush or shrub
with narrow curving leaves, almost without stalks
and set in pairs. It is nearly evergreen, but the
new leaves in May drive out the old. Privet is an
element of chalk scrub, where it tends to need the
protection of other shrubs. It grows in southern
England generally and on the alkaline peat of the
fens. The flowers, white or creamy and heavily

scented, are carried high on the ends of shoots in
pyramid spikes in summer, followed by round
green, then shiny black, berries: poisonous, but
not to the birds. Privet is native here, and in
Europe and N. Africa; related to the ash and the
olive. It is *Ligustrum vulgare*. There are garden
varieties with funny coloured leaves, and the
Japanese and Chinese evergreen privets of
suburban hedges: whether these hybridise with
the common sort I cannot find out.

**Roses** Long trailing stems with strong claw-like
thorns are characteristic of the wild roses, of
which there are dozens of species. The most
common is the dog rose, usually pink flowered.
Downy rose, with down on the leaves, is pinker
flowered, has straight prickles and long bracts
on the round hips: more common in the north.
Field rose is common in woods in the south. It has
slender green stems: southern half of Britain.
Sweet briars resemble the dog rose, but have
flowers and leaves like the downy rose. These are
the commonest. The dog rose and sweet briars
are very much a part of chalk scrub, usually
intertwined with other shrubs, occasionally free

standing, seemingly supported by their own
shoots: sometimes these are vertical, as if waiting
for the wind to decide their direction.

Wild roses are common in hedges: they are
pollinated by bees, wasps and other insects and
their seeds are distributed by the birds. Rose hips
are rich in vitamin C and were gathered during
wartime rationing: they are plentiful for anyone
who likes rose hip jelly, at least as good as most of
the sugary jams in the shops.

*dog rose*

The pretty gall on wild roses is called the robin's pin-cushion, a sickening name. It is caused by the larva of a gall wasp which disrupts the normal development of the bud into filaments instead of leaves. The gall can be inhabited by squatters of different successive species and their parasites, other wasps. The galls are properly known as bedeguars, meaning brought by the wind.

*rose gall*

**Sea Buckthorn** A survivor from the hills of sand and gravel uncovered by the ice, and now covered by other soils – and by the North Sea.

*Hippophae rhamnoides* is common by alpine streams, far from the sea, but in Britain is only found on sand dunes. It is quite rare as a native on the east coast but has been planted in west coast sandy gardens and spread to the dunes; or has been planted on dunes by local authorities to keep the sand from shifting. Here it has benefited from the post-myxomatosis absence of rabbits, who tended to limit the vegetation to short grass.

Sea buckthorn, unlike the common buckthorn, has sharp terminal horns or spines. It is not related and not otherwise similar except that it is a bush with berries, and these are orange, not black. It is said to grow up to a small tree in favoured positions: gardeners plant it for its silvery foliage and rich berries, which are, like rose hips, rich in vitamin C and can be used in marmalade – too acid on their own.

The small green flowers in brown bracts are near the stems, the females singly and the males in clusters, on separate trees. The narrow leaves are blue-green above and grey below, alternate and omnidirectional on the twigs, some of which form spines with vestigial buds and no leaves. The leaves and the bracts of the flowers are covered in minute scales and the berries are dotted on the surface. The colour of the berries, in case the photograph seems to lie, is a strange attractive shade between dull yellow and bright orange.

Old names for sea buckthorn are willow thorn and sallow thorn.

**Spindle**  A shrub of the chalk hills and nearby hedges, the spindle tree is one of three or four plants of scrubland sometimes referred to collectively as dogwood; all used for skewers and all with similar leaves and small green flowers. But in autumn the spindle is quite distinct for its clusters of four-lobed fruit are the only true pink in the landscape. Not content with this, the lobes unfold to show bright orange seed-cases.

The leaves of the spindle are oval, dogwood-style but narrow. In winter the twigs are green and the thin branches have a square section due to ribs in the bark. Whether this made them specially suited to being used as spindles for spinning wool into thread, I do not know. The spindly twigs made, traditionally, the best drawing charcoal: the French name for the spindle tree, *fusain*, also means charcoal.

There are members of the genus *Euonymus* all over the northern hemisphere, usually with the name spindle tree, but one, in the USA, is a Strawberry Bush and another a Burning Bush. Ours, native in southern England and Ireland, is *E.europaeus*.

*wayfaring tree in autumn*

scales, blade-shaped and downy. The mealy terminal bud with folded flower stalks is as if held between two curving leaf buds, like a wafer between wafering irons.

The large, oval, opposite leaves are richly veined, paler and hairy below, and have neatly serrated edges. Flattish clusters of cream-white flowers turn into green berries, ripening patchily, some red, some black. A sickly, rich smell is associated with flowers and fruit, but the latter are taken by the birds, and while the leaves go crimson the stalks of the berry clusters are left like claws. *V. lantana*, once called the hoar-withy, was used to tie up faggots.

Other shrubs in the hedges will usually be escaped from orchards or gardens or planted locally – like the exotic, but naturalised, fuschia hedges of S.W. Ireland.

Tamarisk seems to be almost naturalised on southern coasts, quite recognisable by its feathery foliage. Cherry plums, bullace, and domestic plums can be found growing wild in hedges and more as shrubs than trees.

*spindle flowers*

**Wayfaring tree**  Not known as a tree, but a large bush familiar on chalky waysides, this is a *Viburnum*, similar to garden bushes like *V. tomentosa* and evergreen *V. tinus* (laurustinus). The twigs are warted, like elder, but the buds are immediately recognisable, being without

*fuchsia in the hedge, Kerry*

# 5 – SOME WOODY PLANTS

This is an odd collection: most are bushes; some grow in woods, others form the chief vegetation of their habitat; one is a climber, another sprawls or scrambles, one is a parasite. All have woody, persisting stems and are thus distinguished from herbs. But my list is far from complete. Wild flower specialists will know them all: I have put in only some which could be mistaken for young trees, and some particularly associated with trees.

*catkins of bog myrtle or sweet gale*

**Bilberry,** whortleberry, blaeberry. All the same plant: whortleberry is its southern name. It has bell-shaped or globular, hanging pink flowers in early summer and delicious blue berries, much collected in the N.W. It grows on acid soil in scattered woodland and on banks, heaths and moors. The leaves are light green and deciduous. Cowberry, also a *Vaccinium*, has paler flowers, evergreen leaves and red berries, while Cranberry has very small leaves, odd shaped pink flowers and round dark berries; rather rare.

Bearberry, similar to cowberry, is more restricted to the Highlands, and it creeps or trails over rocks. The even smaller black bearberry of the mountain tops has white flowers.

**Bog myrtle** grows like a miniature forest about three feet high in drier parts of bogs and fens, looking rather like a willow. The spikes of horny catkins appear in April and May before the leaves. The female catkins are smaller, and reddish, on separate plants: small winged fruits follow. The leaves are scented. *Myrica gale*.

**Brambles** or blackberries – about 400 species and hybrids lumped together as *Rubus fruticosa*. Brambles are perhaps the most common

undershrubs in the woods, where they sprawl, rooting at intervals, until a clearing enables them to spread over some support, when they flower and fruit vigorously. Birds carry the seeds to any vacant ground. Left alone in open conditions,

*bramble fills the space round a fallen tree*

**Butcher's broom**  This beautiful example of vegetable unity has no bark or pith and technically no leaves, just leaf-shaped pieces of flattened stem coming to spiny points. It has tiny flowers, not on stalks but in the centres of some leaves, and red berries. It is deep, shiny green, and when a branch dies the sap drains from stem and leaf alike leaving a perfect white ghost. It is native to S.E. England, but was once planted widely for use as – butchers' brooms. Clumps about 2 feet high can be found in woods near old habitations. *Ruscus aculeatus* is a monocotyledon, like palm trees, bamboos, onions and lilies.

brambles with the juiciest berries form thick, crowded bushes. In the hedge they use the support of hawthorn and other shrubs.

All brambles have serrated leaves, sometimes three-lobed, composite in threes and fives. The flowers have five petals and drooping sepals. The stems vary from thorny to very thorny indeed and there are also minute thorns under the leaves. Very commonly the leaves are marked intricately by the larvae of a moth. The caterpillar tunnels inside the leaf, leaving a white track which starts thin and ends thick.

Wild raspberry, *R. idaeus*, has simple leaves, white below. It is not given to clambering like the brambles.

**Currants** (red and black) and gooseberries can be found in the wild, and they were so originally as native plants. They are more likely now to be garden escapes. *Ribes.*

**Heaths** and heather. Heathland and heather moors are dry areas of acid soil. Ling, *Calluna vulgaris,* with spikes of small, pale, purplish-pink flowers and very small leaves, is the commonest. Purple or bell heather is characteristic of drier heaths and moors, and cross-leaved heath of

*cross-leaved heath*

wetter ones. Both these are *Ericas*. There are others, more local. Moors are upland heaths sometimes dominated by grasses – and shading off to moss-dominated bogs where the input of moisture exceeds the output. All heather demands full light. It can develop a tough stem and a low bush form – usually 18 inches is the maximum for British heathers, but an Irish heath grows to 6 feet and the Mediterranean *bruyère* makes a small tree. Heathland in Britain is potential woodland where it is not burnt regularly, taken over by bracken, or overgrazed.

**Honeysuckle** or woodbine is better known for its lovely flowers than for its habit of turning clockwise round young trees, which then grow like corkscrews. It can climb twenty feet or more to the tops of neglected coppices, its stems sometimes hanging as if in a tropical jungle; but it grows mainly in southern hedgerows. It has oval leaves, usually two lots of flowers between June and September, and red berries. Two other common climbers, not woody, are black bryony and white bryony: they also have berries. None of these should be eaten.

**Mistletoe** Parasitic in so far as it roots in trees, usually poplars and apples, tapping their flow of sap, but otherwise growing as a woody plant with green flowers early in the year and juicy, white berries. It is connected with Druidical rites only on the strength of one Roman account. It is the 'thunder-brush' of Sweden. Magic in some vague beneficial way, it is still thought worth hanging over doorways: and kissing under it never did any harm. Very rare in oak trees, limited in northern and western distribution by low summer temperatures. *Viscum album*.

**Spurge laurel** *Daphne laureola*, looks like a young laurel or rhododendron, with leaves clustered at the top of the single, woody stem. It is an evergreen of calcareous woodland with green, petal-less flowers under the leaves in January and February. Black, egg-shaped berries are its poisonous fruits. The English name is descriptive only. Daphnes form a family almost of their own. The other British native is mezereon, deciduous, with fantastic magenta-purple flowers, also in winter, and red berries. It is very rare: too many gardeners.

**Traveller's joy** *Clematis vulgaris* or *vitalba*, is very common in chalk scrub and neglected hedges, where it climbs with the aid of its leaf stalks. These join the stem at strong right-angular joints from where the whitish flowers, on long stalks, bloom in high summer. The seeds form in the centre of masses of hairy feathers, called old man's beard, which in protected places persists through the winter, as in the picture on p. 110. Traveller's joy can climb very high and forms thick fibrous-looking stems. The leaves are compound, of two pairs of opposite leaflets and one terminal, floppy and irregularly oval. Traveller's joy is a member of the buttercup family, Ranunculaceae.

# 6 – PLANTS OF THE WOODS

Any photographer knows that the light within a wood in summer is a small fraction of that outside. The closer the canopy (depending on species and maturity of the trees) the fewer plants are found in the field layer. Since most of our woods are deciduous, plants which leaf and flower early are the general rule: some keep their leaves for most of the year. Most common woodland plants spread more easily by vegetative means, usually underground stems, than by seed, and therefore tend to form continuous drifts.

Bramble, ivy and bilberry are mentioned elsewhere. Bluebells, or wild hyacinths, the best-known known flowers of the woods, need no picture but should be mentioned here: their distribution in and out of the woods is interesting. Nettles, common enough, are not peculiar to woods.

The field layer will revert to grass if the wood is grazed, for grasses grow from the base and thrive on cropping which exterminates other plants.

Rushes and ferns also belong to the field layer and sometimes grow in the trees as epiphytes.

**Foxgloves** are remarkable for their early establishment of rich green leaves before anything else is green and several weeks before the tall flowering spires emerge. They are common in clearings of durmast oak and found in woods and odd corners on acid soil.

**Primroses** are specially associated with recently cut coppice, woodland margins and hedge banks, no less popular for being common, but in places less common because popular. They bloom from March to May. The related cowslip is found in ashwoods in the south, but more often in meadows.

**Wood sorrel** is practically evergreen and peculiarly adapted to pushing its leaves through the dead leaves and twigs of the woodland floor, Very widespread, even in dark beechwoods, it blooms from April to May.

**Sweet woodruff** is larger and has broader leaves than the other bedstraws and goosegrass, which are common in Britain, recognised by leaves in whorls.

**Ramsons,** or wild garlic, can carpet whole woods and copses on damp ground. Leaves are broad and fleshy and aromatic, even underfoot: flowers in May and June.

**Small balsam,** here completely covering the dry soil under a horse chestnut, is an example of a plant which is now increasing its range and frequency from the south-east.

Other balsams are found in clearings, notably the Himalayan balsam, or policeman's helmet.

**Dog's mercury** makes perhaps the commonest woodland plant carpet in England. Noticeable early in the year, in oakwoods and beechwoods and hedge bottoms: it blooms early, in March and April, but stays green all summer. Female plants form seed capsules.

**Rosebay willowherb** colonised the wartime ruins in London and it quickly fills clearings in beechwoods and elsewhere. It is the commonest plant of industrial wasteland yet a hundred years ago it was rare. Other willow-herbs have expanded similarly, particularly along railways.

**Bracken,** the common brake fern, is a useless weed of upland grass and very frequent in heath-land, but kept in check in woodland, where it is always ready to fill a gap – if the soil is acid. It can grow to six feet and it dies down in the winter, smothering tree seedlings.

# 7 - PLANTED TREES

Many familiar trees are planted species which cannot reproduce here from their own seed: others are well on the way to becoming tree-weeds. Here are included, for the sake of completeness, some trees commonly planted for love or gain, but not generally either naturalised or related to native species mentioned in previous chapters.

**Acacia** False acacia, or locust. The original of many an Acacia Avenue, but it is not a member of the Acacia family. It was brought here from N. America, first grown by a Monsieur Robin and named *Robinia pseudacacia*. William Cobbett rediscovered it and popularised it, under the name locust, as a substitute for oak. The trees did not grow well enough here, though they are of major importance in central Europe. Here they remain decorative, occasionally naturalised in warm sandy places, and good town trees. Robinia has soft compound leaves with many oval leaflets, hanging flower clusters and seed pods which show its leguminous nature, and very distinctive bark, like gothic tracery.

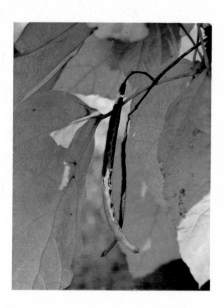

**Catalpa** or Indian bean. The largest leaf, a pointed oval, sometimes lobed here and there; bell-like lobed flowers in clusters; very long seed pods (up to 2 ft). Surprisingly frequent in London: there is one in St James's Churchyard, probably the nearest tree to Piccadilly Circus. *Catalpa bignonioides*, is a native of American deep south riversides, brought here in the eighteenth century.

**Cedars** of Lebanon, Atlas cedars and Deodars. No home was gracious without its cedar of Lebanon – those above are at Chiswick Park, now dwarfing the Italianate, meticulous architecture, their branches swooping round the stone sphinxes on the lawn. Deodars are neater, with triangular sheets of foliage. Atlas cedars, *Cedrus atlantica,* are somewhere between the two, usually enormous, with bushy needles, often greyish. All have erect, massive cones which release their delta-winged seeds from a central core which

*cedars at Chiswick*

remains on the tree. Cedarwood clothes-chests keep the scent of the wood for years.

There are also beautiful Japanese cedars *Cryptomeria;* the western red cedar is a *Thuja* or arbor vitae, with foliage like a cypress.

*Lawson's cypress*

**Cherry Laurel** Strangely leathery for a *Prunus*, this is an Eastern evergreen with regular, tall spikes of flowers in April and egg-shaped, poisonous black cherries. Hedges of it sometimes run wild and smother local vegetation. The very similar, late-flowering, Portugese laurel is also a *Prunus*. Other laurels may actually be Lauraceae, including the well known bay-tree, good for flavouring fish and meat, and crowning poets: *Laurus nobilis*.

**Cypresses** These are many and various. This, above, is a 'false cypress,' *Chamaecyparis lawsoniaria*, the commonest. It is sometimes planted as a forest tree and can reach 200 ft on its home ground, which is the west coast of North America.

**Ginkgo** The representative of a whole group of trees botanically between cycads and conifers, most of them fossilised as coal, *Ginkgo biloba* survived in a remote corner of China. It is much planted in N. America as a street tree and frequently met with here in parks all over the country. The fleshy seeds, if they ripen here, have a nauseous smell and can hurt the skin. The fan-shaped, deciduous leaves can hardly be compared with any other. Gingko was enthusia-stically named the maidenhair tree because the leaf resembles the rare maidenhair fern.

*rudimentary conkers*

**Firs** Fir used to be an alternative name for pine. Now the genus, *Abies*, is properly the silver fir; native to Europe, but not Britain, as *A. alba*. Planted here, the trees proved mostly unresistant to an aphid which normally infests them without much damage. Even so, a silver fir at Inverary was until recently, the tallest tree in Britain, at about 180 ft, the height of Nelson's Column. Instead, *A. grandis* and *A. procera*, both from British Columbia, are planted for their timber – tens of thousands of them every year. The picture above was taken in W. Ross.

The 'Grand' and 'Noble' firs were discovered in 1825 by the Scotsman, David Douglas, whose name was given to the Douglas fir, *Pseudotsuga*. Unlike the silver firs this has hanging cones, recognisable by three-pronged bracts on the scales. Two Douglas firs, having overtaken the silver fir, now compete as the tallest trees in Britain, one in Wales at Powys Castle and another at Dunkeld, Perthshire.

**Horsechestnut** The candelabra of suburban avenues in May and the source of conkers, as well as the sticky buds of youthful botany lessons, this

Balkan tree is well integrated into British life. It is our only tree with large, radiating, compound leaves. The Turks were said, in 1537, to feed the nuts to coughing horses, but horses don't like them; cattle do. Nuts are supposed to grow into seedlings here, but it is very unusual to find a horsechestnut which could not have been planted. The winter silhouette is rather bony and I think we have enough horsechestnuts. *Aesculus hippocastanum* has also some pink-flowered varieties and there are species native to both Japan and China.

**Judas tree** A small tree, not exactly common, but of long residence and rather beautiful. The leaves are very nearly circular. It is a legume and has pea flowers, pink, red or white according to variety (edible in salads as buds) and seed pods. It is surely 'Judea tree' and not the one Judas hanged from – usually said to be the even smaller elder.

**Laburnum** Golden-flowered and three-foliate with poisonous seeds in narrow pods; by every man's front gate. It *can* grow wild and its brown timber is used in musical instruments.

**Larch** Larches are deciduous members of the Pinaceae which I am tempted to say you can recognise by their beauty. However, I will mention the branches drooping at 30° from the horizontal, knobbly twigs, small cones in great quantity. Japanese larches (shown above, near Tring) have smaller cones than the European, and bright, orange-brown twigs in winter. A hybrid between the two seems to have the best features of both from the point of view of timber production, being resistant to both canker and exposure. Before the middle of the eighteenth century larches were planted only for decoration, but landowners discovered that it produced good timber quickly without spoiling their rough shooting – its shade is light. The wood is resinous but makes good poles of all kinds; fences and telegraph poles. It had a special advantage for pit props because it never gave in without a loud warning crack beforehand. High quality larchwood is used in boat building. Hundreds of thousands of acres are under larch in Britain: but it does not do well everywhere and I know a wood of skeleton trees in Derbyshire, extravagantly beautiful even in death. It is sometimes planted with other trees, alternately, for protection.

**Magnolia** Natives of the Far East or the American South, some species have their flowers before the leaves, as early as February. The one above is *Magnolia campbelli*; others have white flowers. All are remarkable for the paucity of invention in their scientific names: one exquisite species, with round, milky petals and crimson stamens, a native of Japan, is called *M. parviflora* or *M. sieboldii*.

**Monkey puzzle** *Araucaria* or Chile pine, has, amongst other benefits, six-inch cones with edible seeds. *A. brasiliensis* gives us 'Parana pine', a hardwood at softwood prices.

135

shaped and familiar in paintings of Italy and Twickenham. It has edible 'pine kernels'.
*P. pinaster*, the maritime or cluster pine, is planted and sometimes naturalised around Bournemouth. Pines with needles in threes are the Californian Monterey pine and pitch pine: long needles, usually bright green.

The Weymouth and Bhutan (Himalayan) pines are hard to tell apart, with long needles in bundles of five and superb long cones. The photograph shows, I think, the Bhutan.

*plane*

**Mulberry** The black mulberry is the only one that does well here, but attempts have been made to cultivate the white mulberry as the food of silkworms. *Morus nigra* belongs to the large and useful family, Moraceae, which contains the figs, rubber-trees, breadfruit and hops. Mulberries in Britain are usually female, grown for their fruit, which is like a superior raspberry, darkening to purple. The tree tends to be squat, with heart-shaped leaves deeply lobed at the stalk and sometimes forming extra lobes in the manner of fig leaves.

**Pines** (See Scots pine, chapter 2) The black pines of Europe have bark similar to the Scots pine but without colour, and egg-shaped cones. Corsican pine is a variety and much planted by the Forestry Commission on sandy and light soils. Another variety is Austrian pine. Lodgepole pine, *Pinus contorta*, from the west coasts of Canada and Alaska, is planted in exposed places on peaty soil in Scotland and Ireland. All these have needles in pairs, as does the distinctive stone pine, umbrella-

**Plane** There are two planes, American and Oriental, and the London plane is a hybrid, *Platanus acerifolia*. The American one, *P. occidentalis* is called there the buttonwood or, confusingly, sycamore. To add to the confusion, the Scots sometimes call the sycamore a plane. *Platanus* and *Acer* are quite distinct and the resemblance between the leaves is very superficial. Planes have bark which peels off decoratively in patches and round fruits of many seeds with individual 'parachutes' of feathers. The flowers, male and female, also take the form of bobbles. London planes usually have two fruiting heads on one stalk, American planes, one, and Oriental planes, several: but this is not a very reliable rule.

The leaves of planes are downy at first. They fall in autumn green from the trees with their hollow stalks, exposing the neat pyramid of next year's bud, surrounded by the leaf scar. Oriental planes are planted in Britain but the hybrid town tree proved so successful, since it was planted in

*young plane trees on the South Bank*

London squares in the eighteenth century, that it was adopted for N. American and European cities. The oldest trees are probably those in Berkeley Square, London, with massive, lumpy boles – and every sign of good health. They were planted in 1789.

The timber of planes used to be called lacewood and was used for fine pieces of furniture.

**Redwoods** A combination of thick red bark and feathery foliage serves to identify the *Sequoia* family: after that it is a little complicated. The tallest forests in the world are Californian redwoods, grown for their timber. There is a plantation at Wilmslow, near Manchester, if that's

any help. A closely related species, *S. gigantea*, is the Big Tree or mammoth tree which holds the world record for thickness (75 ft circumference) and lives three or four thousand years. Somewhat junior specimens here were named (after the Duke) Wellingtonia. Even they have massive hairy trunks, suggesting that mammoth tree is the best name. The leaves of this species are not exactly feathery, being triangular and close to the twig.

A deciduous member of the Sequoias is the swamp cypress or bald cypress. It can actually grow in water. It has a widely buttressed base and sends up root extensions for air.

The Metasequoia or dawn redwood was known as a fossil until 1945, when it was found growing in central China. It has foliage resembling the yew's and, like the redwoods, egg-shaped cones with chunky scales.

**Rhododendrons** Leggy, dusty evergreens of the Victorian shrubbery, but loved by many for their spherical heads of large, funnel-shaped flowers. There are five or six hundred species (including the azaleas, not quite evergreen) and mostly from the Himalayas and S.E. Asia, whence they were first gathered in quantity by the heroic Hookers of Kew. One, *R. ponticum*, with purple flowers, is a native of the Caucasus and Portugal and has become naturalised in Britain. In S.W. Ireland it grows wild from seed (above) but in many parks

137

*rhododendron as shrub layer*

and plantations it just seems to spread, making an alien shrub layer, even under beeches, as above.

**Spruce** *Picea:* pointed trees with pendant cones and needles on pegs. The Norway spruce, well known in juvenile form as the Christmas tree, *P. abies,* was a native of Britain before the last Ice Age. In its natural distribution it avoids mild winters – but it grew alongside oak and pine in our interglacials. Sitka spruce, from sub-arctic Canada, has sharp needles, silvery below, and cones smaller than *P. abies*, with scales thin and wavy-edged. Both these spruces are extensively planted in forests, sitka particularly at a rate which will make it the leading tree in Britain. It produces the fine timber known as silver spruce. Spruce timber generally is called whitewood or white deal (so is that of the silver firs). Paper-making pulp and the raw materials of cellulose products, rayon and some plastics, come from these and other conifers. Spruce forests are dark inside, and they provide a very limited habitat for wild-life mainly because all the trees are the same age and are thinned to just the right distance to make straight timber. But it should be remembered that they mostly replace bare, monotonous peaty moors. The picture is of an oddity, a spruce avenue in Co. Cork.

**Sumach** Small trees native to N. America, China and S. Europe. The one planted in gardens in S. England, for the sake of its brilliant foliage in autumn, is called the Stag's horn sumach because its branches and leaf-stalks are covered with velvety hair. *Rhus typhina* is a near relative of poison ivy.

**Tulip tree** Frequently the centre-piece in lawns of grand houses – this one is at Audley End. They are really tree magnolias from N. America, where they produce a yellow hardwood. Both the leaves and the flowers are tulip-shaped : *Liriodendron tulipifera*

**The tree of heaven** *Ailanthus*, is Chinese and frequently planted in towns. It has large compound leaves spreading palm-like along the branch, the leaflets lobed near the base: small flowers, gold, in July. Occasionally self sown in London.

# 8 - WOODS, FORESTS, PARKS AND TREES

Wild woods are not everyone's favourite places. Perhaps we turn against the scenes of childhood adventures – and early amorous ones: or we are townies and never get over an atavistic fear of nature uncontrolled. Neglected woods can be impenetrable – and that sometimes quite near towns and roads. Recently a complete skeleton, wearing a suit, was found a few hundred yards from a suburb in the south of England. Bits of wooded country everywhere retain more than a hint of the secretive, threatening quality that everyone who, as a child, read of the Wild Wood in *The Wind in the Willows,* recognises at once.

Samuel Bamford, the weaver Radical of Middleton, writing in the early 1840's, describes an old wood in Lancashire – the scene of some innocent black magic organised by his friend Plant, herbalist and amateur magician The wood was in a clough (a rough valley). 'About half way up this kloof... a group of fine oaks appears on a slight eminence, a little to the left. This part of the grove, was, at the time we are concerned with, much more crowded with underwood than at present. The bushes were then close and strong; fine sprouts of 'yerth groon' hazel and ash, were common as nuts; whilst a thick brush of bramble, wild rose, and holly, gave the spot the appearance of a place inclosed and set apart for mysterious concealment. Intermingled

*forest, twenty miles from London*

with these almost impervious barriers, were tufts of tall green fern...' It was the seeds of a fern which were sought for a spell to be cast at midnight, to help the bashful Bangle win his bride.

Edna O'Brien describes in *A Pagan Place* a dark wood on the way to school: 'The ground inside was shifty, a swamp where lilies bloomed. They were called bog-lilies. The donkey went in there to die and no wonder because the shelter was ample. No one would go in to bury it. It decomposed.'

In modern Britain and Ireland the most natural-looking edges of woods are likely to have things dumped in them, not just by passing townies but by farm workers who leave fertilizer bags and tractor oil cans. Nobody cares, unless the wood is for commercial timber or game, or officially recognised as a nature reserve. Even National Trust property is not without its eyesores (and nature-sores) and in places suffers from the wear and tear of too many visitors. 'Take your litter home' plead the notices at beauty-spots: but some of us don't need reminding, while others would rather have a tidy car.

Odd bits of neglected land are the nearest thing to natural woodland (or potential woodland) that most of us can visit frequently, all the year round. Their value should be more appreciated. Some of us must be prepared to take other people's litter home, before local authorities or landowners come along to tidy up and plant neat poplars.

**Forests**

Such fragments of medieval forest as have survived in more than name are now usually more overgrown and mature than when they served the chase and the needs of commoners. Even the great royal forests were largely common land and also contained neat patches of coppice. The greatest is the New Forest, very popular, of course – the verderers' men cheerfully remove thousands of tons of rubbish every year – but rich in every sort of woodland and wild life. The Forest of Dean also contains old oakwoods besides a lot of conifer plantations. Both these large forests are Forest Parks looked after by the Forestry Commission.

Wilderness, with deer as permanent inhabitants, can be found as close to London as Epping Forest, which with Hatfield Forest and Lingwood Common (Chelmsford) are the small remnants of the almost continuous forest which once covered Essex – manorial and royal. The wildest parts of Hatfield Forest are now the overgrown coppices of hazel, hornbeam and wych-elm: the chases are given over to cars and ball games. Hindhead Commons and the Wealden ridge from Holmwood to Hurst Wood in Surrey, and the St Leonard's Forest and Ashdown Forest in Sussex are combinations of heath and oakwood which perhaps come closest to typical 'forest' countryside. The biggest concentration of oaks in Britain is still in Sussex.

Sherwood Forest, parcelled off into the Dukeries and other estates by 'disforestation' in times of royal penury, is no more, except for a few old oaks near Edwinstowe. Sherwood, like Cannock Chase and some other resoundingly named forests and purlieus, is being re-assembled as conifer plantations by the Forestry Commission – twentieth century forests as monuments to medieval ones.

Most of the forests and commons became farms as they were enclosed: odd corners were sometimes left and on the map still show patchily where the old forests were. The lord's demesne, enclosed and protected while the forests were still open, usually became a park – often 'improved' in the eighteenth century by landscape gardening. Such landscaped parks are now very mature – often bordered by old plantations of hardwood trees. Not all, by any means, are open to the public, and this we cannot regret. Managed well for profit they are preserved for the future, without notices and 'toilet facilities'.

*in the Rothiemurchus pine forest; birch and juniper*

## Conifer forests

The Forestry Commission is based in London and is responsible to the Minister of Agriculture and the Secretaries of State for Scotland and Wales. In Eire the Ministry of Lands controls forestry through its Forestry Branch.

The Forestry Commission owns and administers two and a half million acres, about five per cent of Britain. Half a million acres of this is mountain tops and rough grazing. Fifty thousand acres every year are planted with young trees, and fresh land in the hills is held in reserve. Nine-tenths of the Commission's work is with conifers – spruce predominating. Not all the conifer forests in Britain are owned by the Commission: financial help and advice are given to the owners of another two million or so acres. The demand is for softwoods for building and for paper and cellulose. By the end of the century the Commission intends to have five million acres of forest productive. Even so it will not supply a quarter of our needs.

The Irish forests cover three-quarters of a million acres of which eleven per cent is unproductive of trees. The total land has almost doubled in the last ten years. The Irish foresters actually plant broadleaved trees, over five per cent of their total (half of it birch), while the Forestry Commission in Wales plants less than one per cent broadleaves and this is probably typical of the other mountain and woodland area, Scotland. Both the Welsh and Irish plantings consist of 65 per cent sitka spruce. Pines, mostly lodge-pole pine, are planted most in the north-east and south-east of Great Britain and this is broadly true of Eire as well.

In the first years of extensive conifer planting after the war there was a lot of objection from purists concerned to preserve the character of wild

*above: conifers and cloud in central Wales, March*

*Devonshire, early May*

mountain scenery. It was said, rightly in many cases, that the new plantations were too geometrical, and that the alien, uniform trees would poison the soil by blanking out the native flora.

Attempts were made by the foresters to design the outlines in patterns more sympathetic to the sculptured hills, and planning now usually includes patches of grazing and mixed woodland, while much of the high land is dedicated to solitude, not timber production.

The immense conifer forests seem sometimes oppressive, sometimes simply impressive. As the trees grow large we see their real beauty, and though the habitat they provide is meagre the roadsides and rides can be as fascinating as the hedges in the lowlands. Deer use the forests as private corridors, and in Ireland feral goats are reported.

If and when some industrial substitute kills the demand for softwood the ecological problem will be a nice one. Are the miles of alien trees as unstable as we might be led to think by the often-mentioned dangers of fire and insect and fungal attack? What would be the pattern as the planted conifers died and native trees began to colonise?

**Landscape with trees**
The greater part of Britain is of course farmed. The picture above can perhaps stand for a sort of ideal lowland countryside. It was taken in 1971. Wooded hills, moorland beyond: a pattern of smallish fields liberally bordered with hedges and trees, intersected by quiet lanes, with graceful homesteads at distant intervals. It's nearly perfect: and depends for this largely on the rich variety of smallish trees which are of no great value to the farmer except for incidental timber and shelter for his beasts.

143

*Hyde Park, August evening*

Often the trees border a stream or drain and shelter a rich variety of herbs. A mixture of ash, oak, elm, sallows, elder, sycamore and thorns, the trees are there partly as the remains of old woodland, some planted, some not. The holly at the left is in someone's garden, with orchard trees beyond.

The triangle of heathy land near the centre of the picture, with gorse scrub, is characteristic of moorland edges – this is the eastern side of Dartmoor. Such corners, not necessarily ill-drained, are to be found all over Britain – even in towns, by railway sidings and at the edges of factory estates: you can think of at least one. These are potential wild nature reserves – mini-reserves – which, if left, will turn into woodland of one sort or another. Educationally, aesthetically and ecologically they are needed. They should be enclosed for several years until well enough grown to avoid casual car parking and dumping of rubbish.

## Parks

London is blessed with many parks and squares, especially in the central area – and even the outskirts, which have their open spaces, have parks as well. Every town and city in the kingdom has parks, usually to be proud of. Some naturalists, tied to town by their jobs, manage to record surprising totals of birds and other fauna in municipal parks that are everything but nature-reserves. As for the trees, what they lack in wildness they often make up in strangeness. Not a few town parks are the survivors of well-planted estates, marooned amongst the streets.

Miles Hadfield remarks in *Discovering England's Trees* that the only book on London's park trees is over half a century old. Its author, Webster, counted 220 distinct kinds of tree in Kensington Gardens – Hyde Park alone.

From the large free-standing figs in St James's to the swamp cypress in the Serpentine there is obviously plenty of interesting material. The Stationery Office publishes reports on trees in certain parks.

Further out, there are superb trees at Greenwich, Hampton Court, Osterley, Syon (and Kew need not be mentioned). Mature birchwoods at Wimbledon and Hampstead are somewhere between parks and wild land (occasionally the scenes of human nastiness). There are hints of real forest at Kenwood and Richmond. There is a corporation nature reserve at Surbiton: The Wood. But even tiny municipal parks may contain fine specimen trees, worth looking at.

## Arboreta

Tree collections started by Victorian enthusiasts are branches of gardening and nothing much to do with trees in the wild. They tend to emphasise the more exotic conifers and rhododendrons, and can cause claustrophobia. Still, you can't be interested in trees without admiring all trees, and it is worth remembering that many Californian, Chinese and Japanese trees were first being discovered during the last century by European travellers. The transport of seed to British gardens and the raising of trees (which may now be giants) was pioneering work. Unusual varieties of familiar species are another feature of tree collections.

Three important arboreta are now run by the Forestry Commission: at Westonbirt, Gloucestershire, the greatest for conifers and broadleaves; at Bedgebury, Kent, a pinetum and trial forest plots; and close to the Argyll forest park at Kilmun, where several eucalyptus species have been·raised in an unlikely environment. There are euculyptus too at the John F. Kennedy Park in Co. Wexford (actually there are some 'wild' ones near Youghal).

A famous collection is at Sheffield Park, Sussex, with a series of Capability Brown lakes and even some palms. This garden is owned by the National Trust – as is Stourhead, even more famous. Two, out of many, National Trust gardens that combine sub-tropical lushness and Atlantic magnificence are Bodnant, Denbighshire and Glendurgan, Cornwall. Bicton, Devon, has a fine Pinacea collection, with an avenue of monkey trees: there is another at Glendalough, Co. Wicklow. The most extraordinary garden in Britain is probably that of Tresco Abbey, Scilly, with many sub-tropical trees.

## Forest Parks

The Forestry Commission and the Irish Forestry Branch take great pains to welcome the public and inform them of amenities. Recreation is regarded as a proper form of land use, and particularly in the New and Dean Forests the Commission has an important social function, not merely an agricultural one. In the great Forest Parks in Scotland, Wales and the Border country, and also in plantations of 2,000 acres or more dotted over the whole of England the Commission is benevolent in attitude, particularly to those who go on foot. Publications are free or very cheap (see page 147). An Irish booklet called *The Open Forest* is published free and lists 280 forest areas open to the public.

Apart from the great New and Dean forests, which do have large areas of conifers, the Forest Parks are enormous aggregates of conifer plantations with special facilities for tourists and campers. They are mostly close to or contained in National Parks, and are among magnificent scenery. The Border Forest Park with the adjoining Northumberland National Park is the largest new plantation area – nearly 300 square miles includes the old forests of Kielder, Wark, Redesdale and Harwood and several others on both sides of the border.

Queen Elizabeth Forest Park, 41,500 acres, lies between Loch Lomond and the Trossach peaks. The Argyll National Forest Park, nearly 60,000 acres, is to the west of Loch Long. Glen Trool, much more than a glen, is well over 100,000 acres with Merrick (2,764 ft) in the centre and reaching south to Newton Stewart, east to New Galloway and north to the Ayrshire forests of Carrick, Tairlaw and Changue.

The important mountain areas of Cairngorm and Snowdon have Forest Parks as part of the complex of nature reserves, climbing and tourism generally. The Cairngorm National Nature Reserve adjoins the Glenmore Forest Park, approached via the concrete oasis of Aviemore. The Snowdonia Forest Park is patched and integrated into the National Park, mainly to the east of the Snowdon range, with a smaller, (four square miles) plantation on the Beddgelert side and large forests southwards below Cader Idris and just off the National Park at Lake Vyrnwy. Other forestry areas in Wales are grouped near Aberystwyth (Cambrian Forests) and Swansea (Glamorgan Forests) the latter mainly in the foothills of the Brecon Beacons. Other important plantations are in England at Cannock Chase, Staffordshire; Thetford Chase, Norfolk; and, mostly privately owned, in the North York Moors. And, as I mentioned earlier, in nearly every county in England.

**Nature reserves**

National Nature Reserves totalling 300,000 acres are managed by the Nature Conservancy, 19 Belgrave Square, London SW1, a Government body which will give the addresses of Regional Officers who must be approached for permits. The point of a nature reserve is protection, and people are welcome only on certain conditions. Some of the National reserves are Forest (or woodland) Reserves while others which may be important for particular tree species or types of woodland are run primarily for the sake of their animal life. The Shell Guide listed opposite will help – it has excellent maps. This Guide also lists addresses of county Naturalists' Trusts, which usually own and administer several nature reserves in their own areas. Fitter's *Finding Wild Flowers* also gives these and other addresses and contains a most useful guide to woodlands, county by county, as well as helping to find and identify wild flowers, shrubs and trees.

My favourite nature reserves are neglected corners in town and country which are administered by nobody. My advice is: start where you are, and get to know your own bit. It may turn out to be just as interesting as a famous piece of country 50 miles away.

If you like societies, join your local natural history society – secretary's address from the reference library or from the Council for Nature, The Zoo, Regent's Park, London NW1. Best of all, do something really useful; join your nearest Conservation Corps, address from the National Conservation Corps, again at the Zoo, London NW1. There's no time like now.

*eucalyptus trees in the wilds of County Cork*

# BOOKS

Harold C. Bold   *The Plant Kingdom*   Prentice Hall 1970
*Chambers' Pocket Herbal*   1800
Stella Ross-Craig   *Drawings of British Plants*   Part XXVII (80p) etc   Bell 1970
A. Darlington   *The World of a Tree*   Faber 1972
H. L. Edlin   *Trees, Woods and Man*   Collins New Naturalist 1956
           *Know Your Broadleaves*   HMSO 1971 (80p)
           *Know Your Conifers*   HMSO (30p)
Forestry Commission Booklets (and free leaflets) available from the Forestry Commission,
   25 Savile Row, W.1 and Government Bookshops
James Fisher   *Shell Nature Lovers' Atlas*   Ebury Press & Michael Joseph 1966 (40p)
R. S. R. Fitter   *Finding Wild Flowers*   Collins 1971
H. Godwin   *History of the British Flora*   Cambridge 1956
Miles Hadfield   *British Trees*   Dent 1957
           *Discovering England's Trees*   Shire Publications 1970 (25p)
Rev. C. A. Johns   *Forest Trees of Britain*   1846
F. K. Makins   *The Identification of Trees and Shrubs*   Dent 1947
Winifred Pennington   *History of British Vegetation*   English Universities Press 1969
F. H. Perring & S. M. Walters   *Atlas of the British Flora*   Nelson 1962
The Reader's Digest   *Complete Atlas of the British Isles* 1965
A. G. Tansley   *Britain's Green Mantle*   Allen & Unwin 1968
           *The British Isles and their Vegetation*   Cambridge 1939
J. H. Wilkes   *Trees of the British Isles in History and Legend*   Muller 1972

# INDEX

## main entries in bold type

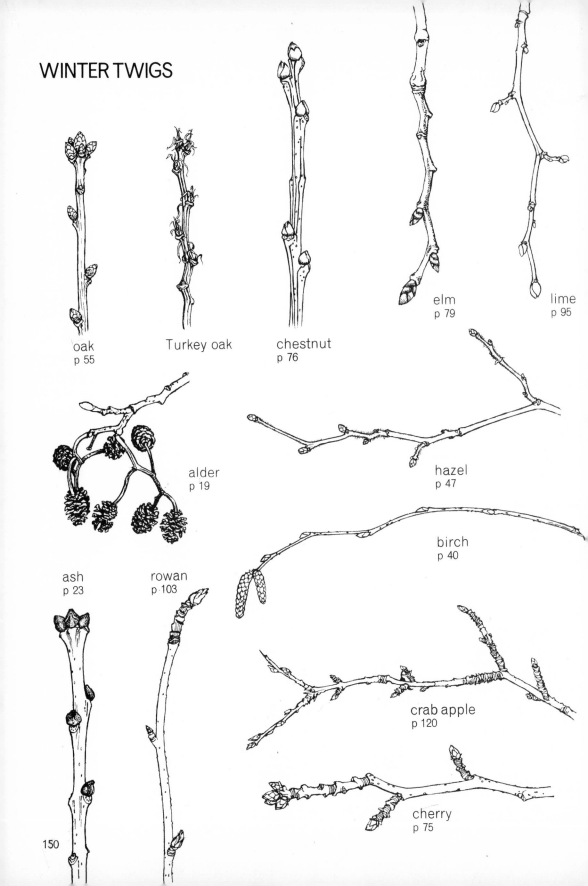

# WINTER TWIGS

oak
p 55

Turkey oak

chestnut
p 76

elm
p 79

lime
p 95

alder
p 19

hazel
p 47

birch
p 40

ash
p 23

rowan
p 103

crab apple
p 120

cherry
p 75

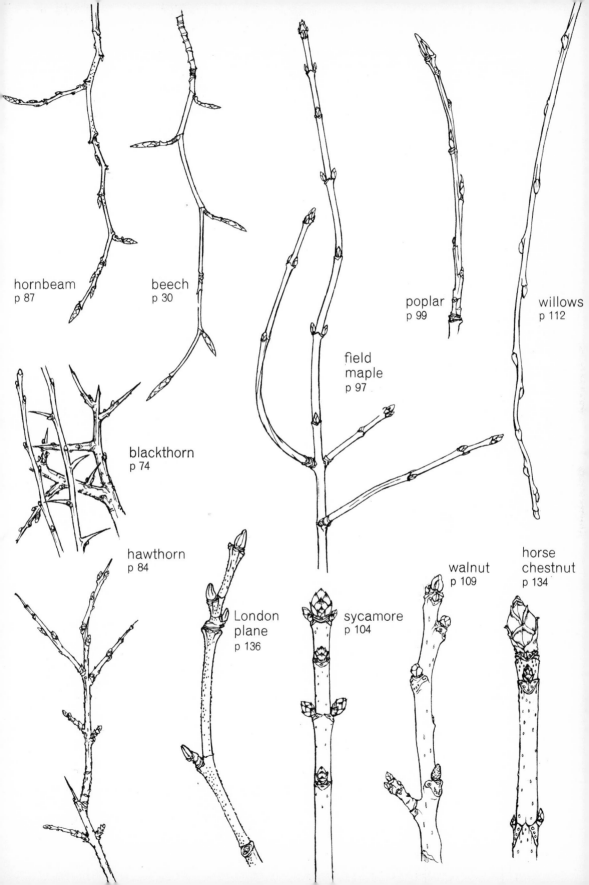

hornbeam
p 87

beech
p 30

poplar
p 99

willows
p 112

field
maple
p 97

blackthorn
p 74

hawthorn
p 84

London
plane
p 136

sycamore
p 104

walnut
p 109

horse
chestnut
p 134

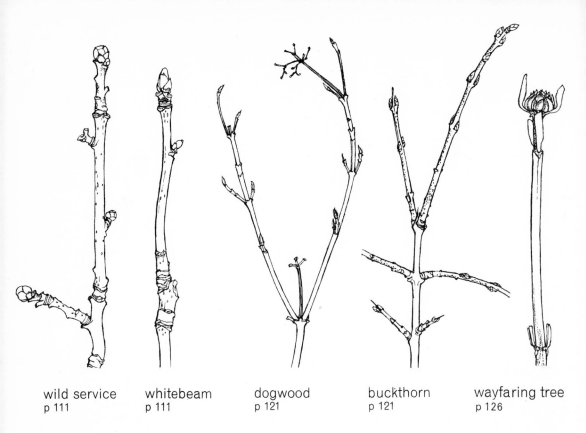

| wild service | whitebeam | dogwood | buckthorn | wayfaring tree |
|---|---|---|---|---|
| p 111 | p 111 | p 121 | p 121 | p 126 |

*winter twigs of the chalk*

# LEAVES OF DECIDUOUS TREES

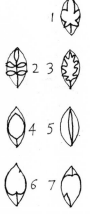

The following leaf charts are arranged as a visual index. Starting with three- and five-lobed leaves (maple-like) we progress to composite ones (like ash). Oval, many lobed leaves follow, centred on oak. The next two facing pages are of oval, usually pointed, shapes, from the spiny chestnut, nearest to the oak, to the narrow sea buckthorn and willows. The last two pages deal with heart-shaped leaves such as lime, ending with circular and two-lobed.

There are many omissions. The simply oval, pointed bird cherry must stand for a whole series of Rosaceae, which would all have looked the same in this context. By their fruits ye may know them. You will find, in parks and gardens, many beautiful leaves not in this chart. The best reference book is that by Makins (see p 147), with diagrams and descriptions of more than 1800 species.

I hope you will enjoy getting to know the trees as much as I do. One thing is certain: there is no point at which you can say, I have finished.

tulip tree
p 138

guelder rose
p 122

fig
p 145

field maple
p 97

maple
p 98

sycamore
p 104

London plane
p 136

currant
p 128

wild service
p 111

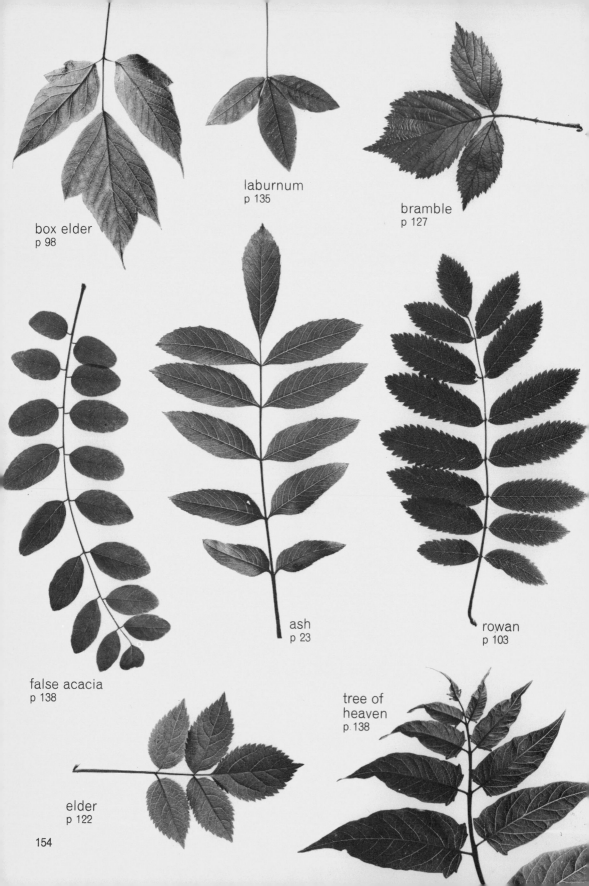

box elder
p 98

laburnum
p 135

bramble
p 127

false acacia
p 138

ash
p 23

rowan
p 103

tree of
heaven
p 138

elder
p 122

154

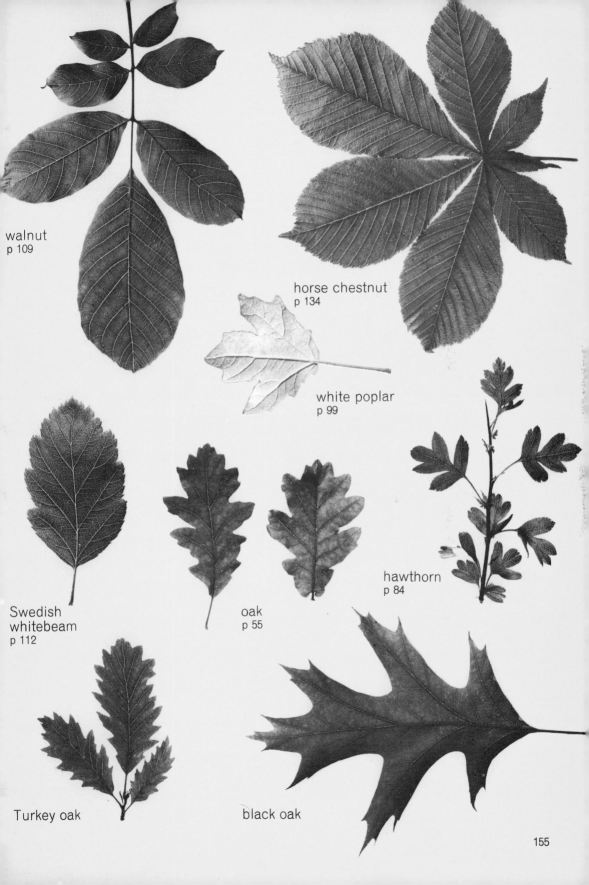

walnut
p 109

horse chestnut
p 134

white poplar
p 99

Swedish
whitebeam
p 112

oak
p 55

hawthorn
p 84

Turkey oak

black oak

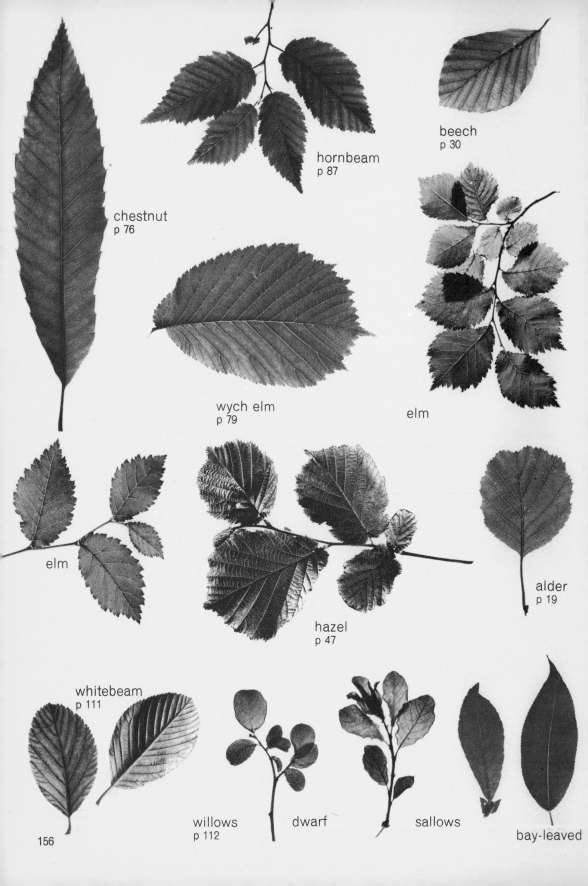

hornbeam
p 87

beech
p 30

chestnut
p 76

wych elm
p 79

elm

elm

hazel
p 47

alder
p 19

whitebeam
p 111

willows
p 112

dwarf

sallows

bay-leaved

156

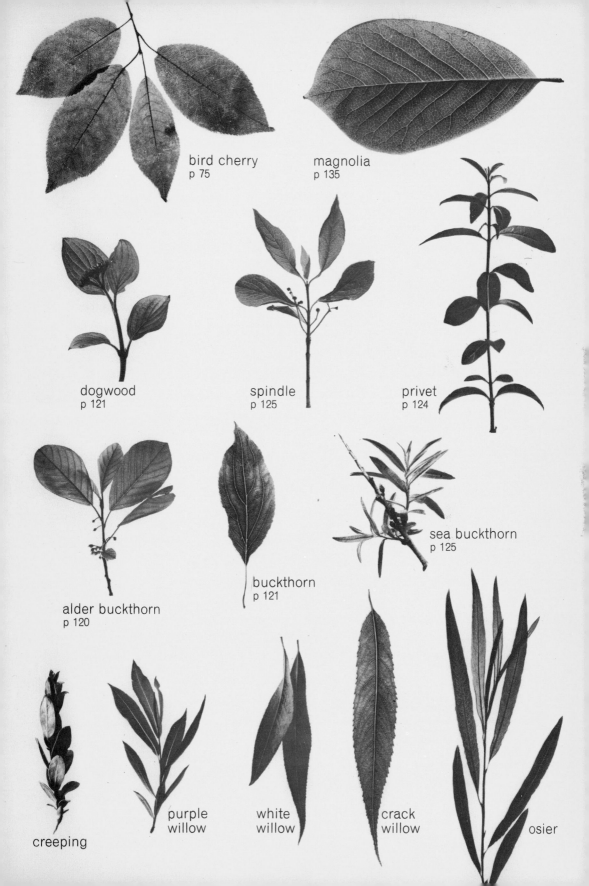

bird cherry
p 75

magnolia
p 135

dogwood
p 121

spindle
p 125

privet
p 124

alder buckthorn
p 120

buckthorn
p 121

sea buckthorn
p 125

creeping

purple
willow

white
willow

crack
willow

osier

Canadian poplar

black poplar
p 99

grey poplar

lime
p 95

black mulberry
p 136

aspen
p 99

alder
p 19

birch
p 40

dwarf birch

judas tree
p 134

gingko
p 133